ON THE NATURE OF THINGS

GAVIN KEENEY

ON THE NATURE OF THINGS

CONTEMPORARY AMERICAN LANDSCAPE ARCHITECTURE

WITH FOREWORDS BY
JOHN DIXON HUNT AND
ALLEN S. WEISS

Birkhäuser – Publishers for Architecture
Basel · Berlin · Boston

A CIP catalogue record for this book is available from the Library of Congress, Washington, D.C., U.S.A.

Deutsche Bibliothek Cataloging-in-Publication Data

Keeney, Gavin:
On the nature of things : contemporary American landscape architecture /
Gavin Keeney. With forewords by John Dixon Hunt and Allen S. Weiss. -
Basel ; Boston ; Berlin : Birkhäuser, 2000
ISBN 3-7643-6192-1

Layout and Cover Design: Muriel Comby

Printed on acid-free paper produced from chlorine-free pulp. TCF ∞
Printed in Germany

ISBN 3-7643-6192-1

9 8 7 6 5 4 3 2 1

CONTENTS

SIGNIFICANCE WITHIN THE ORDINARY

The great modern American poet, Wallace Stevens, makes no appearance in these pages. Yet his dialogic concern with poetry / "imagination" and prose / "reality" haunts most of the selected sites and designs and underlies Gavin Keeney's exegesis of them. On the one hand is landscape architecture's dedication to "pure reality, untouched by trope or deviation", expressed in the language of everyday, the vulgar tongue, or what Stevens famously called the "vulgate of experience". On the other hand is the poetic translation of that "plain version" of things seen into the creative, "Latin" tongue that celebrates the uncommon, the unexpected and unnoticed, the *jouissance* in our experience of things.

Contemporary landscape architecture, making its turn into a new century, seems concerned to move beyond both tenets that have guided its modernist phase (quantitative analysis, ecological deference to natural cycles) and older concerns with picturesque, scenic and pastoral values (Frederick Law Olmsted stills seems to epitomize these for his fellow Americans). A move, too, beyond formalism signals designers' unease with both the mere surfaces of things and their aestheticisation. The firms featured here, however different at first sight, seem to share concerns for strategies that will reconnect, without glossing over, the prose of their world with its poetry: designers display a renewed dedication to the theatrical potential of their sites, to the interactivity to be generated there – both physical (how visitors can be moved through spaces) and metaphysical (how visitors will be moved whether to tears, to laughter or to intuit a world of allusions beyond the first forms they encounter). Designers strive to avoid "averageness", a bland submission to the demands of economy or politics; instead they engage with the given context (in particular, displaying infrastructures not hiding them away), with the challenge of assembling forgotten or fresh ensembles, with convening "significance within the ordinary".

Contemporary landscape architecture is also concerned, with good reason, to defend itself against charges of anti- or un-intellectualism. Its endeavours here provoke a different sort of reflection on the poetry / prose dialogue. On the one hand, the world needs its prose as well as its poetry, as

Stevens knew, and not every utterance – or design – can aspire to a density and connotative depth that we expect from poetry. But, on the other hand, as Stevens also knew, there was good prose and bad prose. That should give readers of this book pause to ask whether there is not room for good "prose" design that an excess of poetic regard for "conceptual and artistic" display is liable to miss (Bryant Park, perhaps, *pace* Keeney).

Another challenge for readers will be to connect the imagery and careful description of actual sites, offered in the first and third sections, with the claims that the author makes for their larger endeavours in the second. We might phrase this problem as: how does the experience, the "consumption", of any one of these sites intersect with the theoretical ambitions that apparently drive this group of designers? Not simply, do we recognize the gardens of Dumbarton Oaks slyly hidden in Keeney's hypothetical garden of Pascal (p. 90); but should we think, equally, of Pascal when we pause in that magical Ellipse by Beatrix Farrand? And, incidentally, given the contemporary focus of this book, why do we need to invoke that (admittedly exemplary) American garden to instance the fresh dialogue of form with idea today?

Here we confront once again our need for narratives and theories of the reception of landscape architecture as well as histories of its design. We desperately need to test whatever claims are made for new work by critics or by designers themselves against the recurring and repeated experiences of those who visit them. Keeney here renders us the great service of setting out the ambitions and the claims that can be made for a series of recently built or projected sites. We shall have time to inhabit them and to meditate on them and within them. And if they indeed constitute "universal figures", metaphors for all time, then we shall have learnt to make sense of their provocations and idealizations, their cultural debts and their philosophical promises.

A LANDSCAPE MANIFESTO

Some time ago, a review of my book *Mirrors of Infinity* ended with what has become a common refrain in contemporary criticism, bemoaning the "abyss between practice and academia" (usually generalized as the rift between theory and practice). The review concluded with the vituperative criticism that such writing creates an identity crisis in the profession of landscape architecture, and that *Mirrors of Infinity* "will only deepen this identity crisis." I would like to take those words and offer them in turn to Gavin Keeney, as a true compliment regarding writing on landscape, for what more can one wish than to revivify an academic field by provoking a crisis!? Situating landscape architecture at the intersection of philosophy, science and art, Gavin Keeney explains that "this epistemological essence is both the promise and the curse of design languages". In his hands, it is a promise beginning to be fulfilled. For he fully realizes that the design elements of landscape architecture must be supplemented by precisely those phantasmatic activities that add moments of "perverse charm to the static, homogeneous everyday experience of the world", moments of "disorder, distemper, disease and dystopia". Motivated by this expanded perspective on landscape, I would like to offer the following manifesto:

The garden is a symbolic form.
The garden contains other symbolic forms.
The garden is a gesamtkunstwerk.
The garden is a synaesthetic matrix.
The garden is a memory theater.
The garden is a narrative, a transformer of narratives, and a generator of narratives.
The garden is a hyperbolically ephemeral structure.
The garden is simultaneously a hermetic space and an object in the world.
The garden is a paradox, combining mathematics and magic, history and myth, science and art, reality and utopia.
The unpeopled garden is either an abstraction or a ruin.

Gavin Keeney's meditations on landscape might well be situated in the lineage of Robert Smithson's theory and practice of the late 1960s. Minimalist and post-minimalist land art was informed by radical reconsiderations of the roles of entropy, ruin, extra-human scale, cosmic temporality, utopianism, mythology, infinity, the void, the cinematic, the gallery, and the complex interrelations between the arts. This nexus of discourse and praxis should be recognized as marking a paradigm shift in the history of landscape architecture, one summed up by Gavin Keeney's claim that, "Landscape architecture, in its highest modality, might be conceived as a series of gestures that seeks to revivify entropic states." Indeed, consideration of the "entropic disorders of the natural world" reveal that the uncanny and sublime within the landscape is not merely an abstract matter. We might well remember the storms that ripped through France in December 1999, destroying over 10 000 trees in Versailles alone. The "Cartesian" garden was inexorably traumatized and transformed by this sublime manifestation of nature, this most violent of entropic events, invoking the existential anguish that underlies the fascinating charms of gardens. And it should be stressed that these events were not accidental, but essential to the very form of Versailles. Such should serve as an allegory, and a warning. The value of Gavin Keeney's writing is that it is sensitive to both those charms and that anguish – an anguish without which the art of landscape architecture can never address the social difficulties and ecological catastrophes that the pleasures of gardens can in some small part assuage.

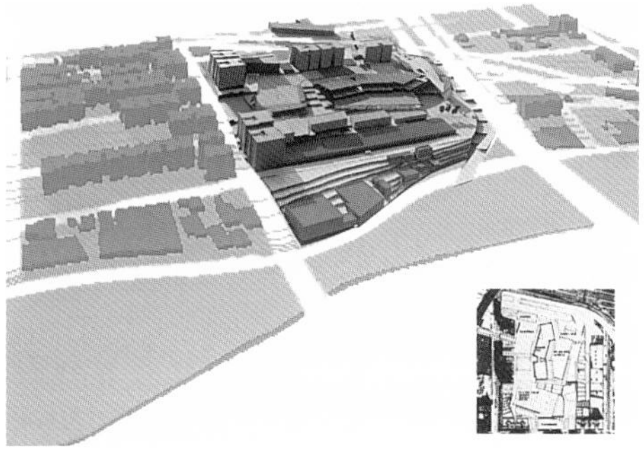

1

2

MARPILLERO POLLAK ARCHITECTS – NEW YORK

URBAN MORPHOLOGY

In their implicit critique of abstract urban planning, Marpillero Pollak Architects envision complex, heterogeneous urban landscape that integrates function, social ambiance, architecture and landscape through the subtle manipulation of scales and the layering, inversion and metamorphosis of historical and formal frames of reference. As urban morphological studies, their projects range from seemingly ordinary master-planning initiatives to intimate site-specific entourage. The result is both polemical and constructive urban interventions that weave together disparate aesthetic and environmental conditions. In site-specific examples, a complex organization with multiple systems and artistic detailing yields new public urban facilities for flexible activity contrary to the empirical impositions of urban planning based on either sociological or purely aesthetic precepts. The perceptual concepts of "reflective" natures and "virtual" natures return in projects in both urban and extra-urban settings.

Marpillero Pollak projects range from urban remediation (mapping and channeling urban forces) to environmental design at a local, contextual level – projects ranging from the strategic to the contingent. Grants for urban design studies have fueled the polemical nature of many of the current built works. "Building Public Space: Questions, Paradigms, Strategies" (1992–1993), a two-year, twelve-city exhibition sponsored by *Progressive Architecture* magazine and ADPSR (Architects Designers and Planners for Social Responsibility) and "Beyond the Box: Notes on Building City Landscape" (1995) both inform their current design.

The structural logic of the proposals is established by analysis of economic, environmental and social factors without a de-naturing descent into purely quantitative methodologies. "Site as pro-

1
Beyond the Box,
New York City, NY,
volumetric study

2
Building Public Space,
"infrastructures",
model

3
Elevated Train Stations,
Hatta, Nagoya, Japan,
section/elevation

4
Elevated Train Stations,
canopy and garden
photomontage

gram" is the hallmark of their enlightened contextualist approach to urban space. An ecology of measures creates a set of interdependent figurative and concrete urban factors and thus provides an atmospheric boon – a surplus of meanings, associations and indeterminate elements. This by-product in turn becomes a chief constituent of the heterogeneous paradigm. A *mise-en-scène* sensibility applied to urbanism, the strategy liberates an active matrix of unstable conditions and epi-phenomena consistent with Artaud's critique of theater as an art form that is impoverished by an emphasis on foreground or dialog at the expense of everything else.

As the result of a close reading of urban form, morphology is predicated on responding to real and hypothetical variables. Marpillero Pollak's study "Beyond the Box" was part of a successful public campaign to defeat the proposed re-zoning of New York City industrial zones to allow large-scale retail development. It examined the implications of the controversial 1995 plan for superstores in post-industrial New York City neighborhoods. The 200000-sq.-ft. superstore (with acres of parking) planned for down-at-the-heels parts of New York City failed to account for the environmental impact within complex, mixed-use communities. "Scales of difference" became the organizational tool for the architectural deconstruction of this typology and for the substitution of subsequent alternative schemes. Scaling ideas (local and global), based on ideas derived from Henri Lefèbvre's *The Production of Space*, were applied to the superblock phenomenon, a remnant of 1960s urban planning. This critical reading introduces the notion of multiple identities versus the monolithic sameness of the superblock.

The breakup of the monolithic is the chief outcome of the pursuit of the heterogeneous in landscape and architecture. Approaches, openings and infiltration of landscape occur at different scales and levels. Implicit hierarchy is often inverted. Countering the pastoral idiom of much urban landscape (the so-called Either/Or approach), the resultant insinuation of nature and green space (gardens) into such urban environments (superblock, mega-structure or urban infrastructure) requires a cultured, streamlined and modest deployment of ambiance versus the universalizing sameness of the traditional urban park. This urban landscape is the ultimate synthesis of the age-old dialectic of nature/culture – it is the architectural landscape garden.

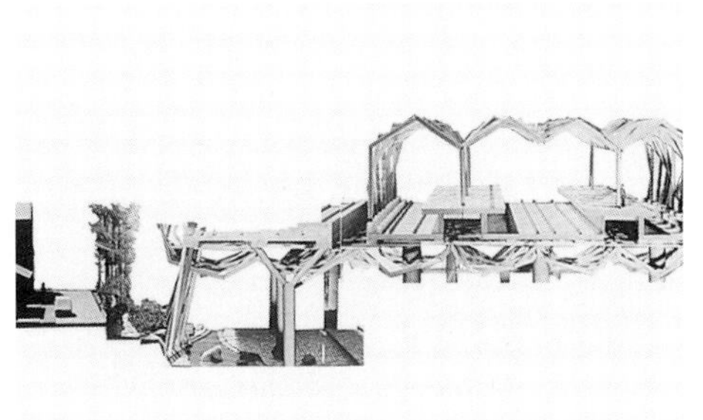

3

4

12

6

PETROSINO PARK — NEW YORK CITY

A leftover traffic island in SoHo, the existing Petrosino Park is roughly 160 ft.×40 ft. Triangular in plan, its north end is squeezed by the convergence of two streets. Its south end bears traces of its role as a memorial garden and small municipal park. The history of the site is one of progressive isolation – the addition of new streets and sub-grade infrastructure – with the end result an island floating amid asphalt and concrete.

Marpillero Pollak's plan establishes "four urban thresholds": 1/overlook walkway; 2/Petrosino Square; 3/market-porch and 4/Petrosino Garden/Subway Entrance. Miniaturized landscape types (traces of an imagined larger order) are proposed for the island-park, including orchard trees, grass steps and garden. A reflective wall (a device that would be both illusionistic and practical) is used to double the spatial experience, as is common in small New York restaurants. A market-porch on the west edge would embrace the SoHo side of this urban gray zone or threshold. A "brick hill" as plaza would provide a topographic essence related to obliterated block patterns. The tiny park gains stature by vertical and horizontal layers that connect back to the surrounding fabric.

5
Petrosino Park,
SoHo, New York City, NY,
schematic collage

6
Petrosino Park,
views of garden
landscape

7
Petrosino Park,
site plan

8
Petrosino Park,
perspective of overlook
walkway

9
Petrosino Park,
urban layers
axonometric

10
Petrosino Park,
aerial view,
photomontage

8

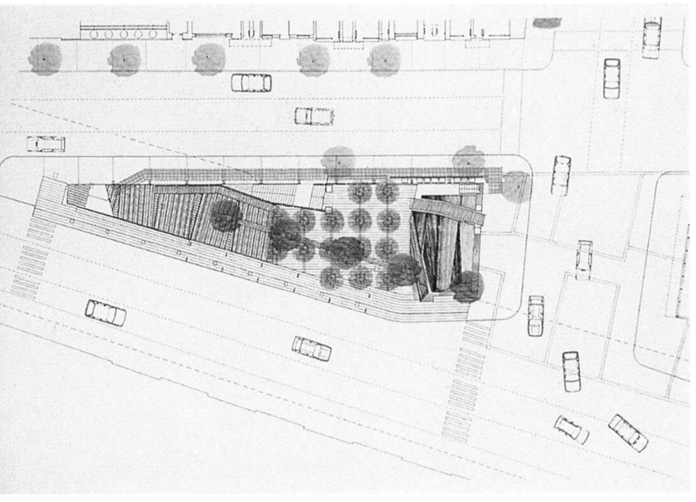
7

9

10

11

BCA SPACE — BOSTON

Intended to serve as a neighborhood park *and* – simultaneously – a parking lot, BCA Space adjoins an arts center in Boston's South End. Surrounded by derelict and, therefore, potentially picturesque buildings, BCA Space exists at the intersection of commercial and civic real estate ventures.

Marpillero Pollak's project utilizes the extant parking pattern to scale and organize the new programmatic elements of the cultural park. As car park / park, BCA Space has a dual identity that is inherently problematic. Its ground – asphalt – and its geometry – trapezoidal – further complicated its intended transformation to an arts facility. By developing a time-lapse program (weekday noon, weekday, evening 1, evening 2) the Marpillero Pollak plan creates "partially open spaces" based on the time of day and week. Temporality is privileged versus the static timelessness of most public urban spaces (e.g. Boston City Hall Plaza).

Virtual landscape (e.g. Jennifer Bloomer's "hypertextual picturesque") supplies additional ambiance by way of back-lit translucent panels (a variation on urban advertising). An outdoor cinema is the prime event horizon for evenings in the park. A *mise-en-scène* sensibility is palpable yet understated (given the parking grove and industrial milieu).

11
BCA Space, Boston, MA, model view

12
BCA Space, exploded axonometric

13 | 14
BCA Space, virtual landscape installations, photomontages

12

13

14

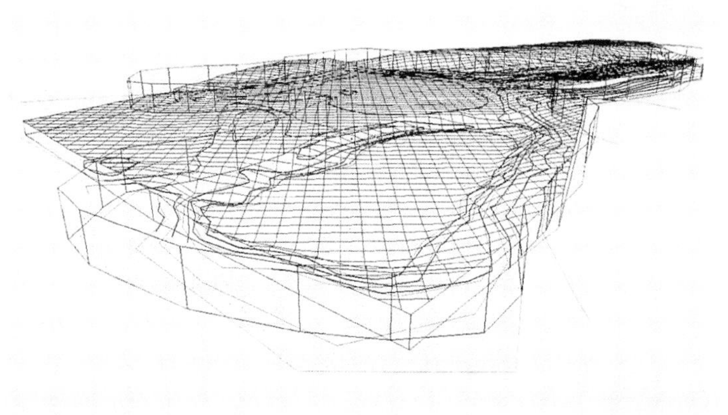

15

16

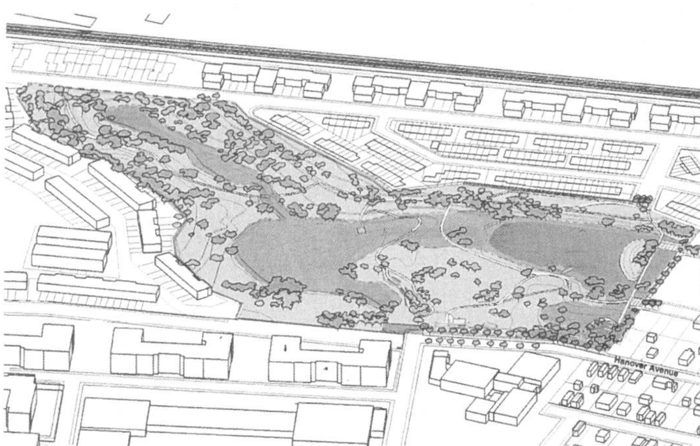

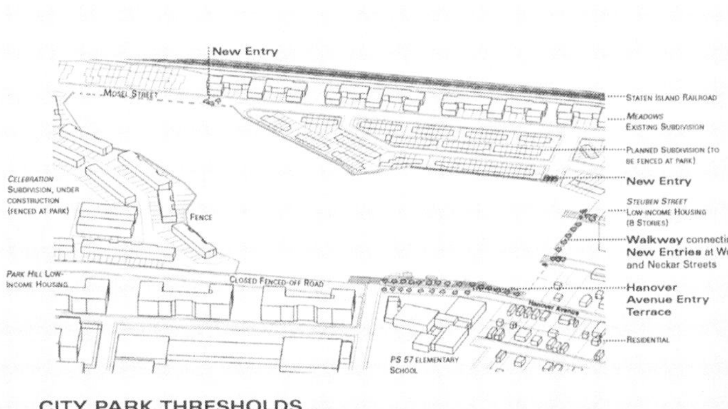

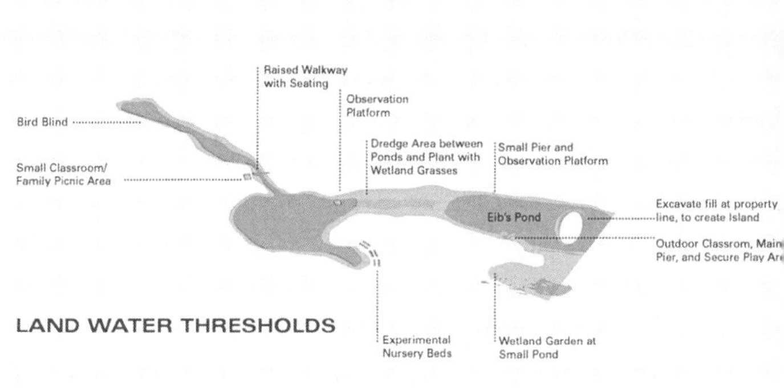

17 | 18

19 | 20

21

22

EIB'S POND PARK — STATEN ISLAND

Eib's Pond Park is a half-pastoral composition. A former dilapidated swamp and accidental junkyard, it is in the process of becoming a 17-acre outdoor classroom and neighborhood wetland park. Its low-income environs and its pastoral history (as part of a 19th-century farmstead) clash in the purposeful evocation of both its agricultural and urban incarnations.

Intended as a functioning wetland, the park will be re-colonized with "boundary events" – walkways, platforms, learning stations – and wild nature. The Hanover Avenue entry plaza is the most architectonic aspect of the planned makeover. It includes a multi-level terrace with thematic installations, a pavilion and a freestanding pergola. The street wall is built up with gabion stone barriers and street trees above. The terrace is opposite a public school. Despite the intervention of Hanover Avenue, it reads as an extension into the park of the school facility. Four other entrances to the park diffuse pressures on the south entry plaza.

Within the park proper water and vegetation are primary with lyrical, low-tech bridges, walkways and pavilions sprinkled about the corridors and meadows. These appurtenances substitute for the usual visual icons of parks – statues and other art objects. They are of an intentionally diminutive scale. The removed junk (tires, automobiles etc) and the restored vegetation bracket the conditional nature of the park. A statuesque egret or heron will also substitute for the normative art object as exclamation point.

15
Eib's Pond Park, Staten Island, NY, topographic wireframe

16
Eib's Pond Park, aerial view

17
Eib's Pond Park, axonometric plan

18
Eib's Pond Park, Landscapes Between

19
Eib's Pond Park, City Park Thresholds

20
Eib's Pond Park, Land Water Thresholds

21
Eib's Pond Park, Hanover Avenue, entry plaza

22
Eib's Pond Park, entry plaza view, photomontage

23

24

25

23
Eib's Pond Park,
restored marsh

24
Eib's Pond Park,
classroom,
photomontage

25
Eib's Pond Park,
view to Park Hill Housing

MARPILLERO POLLAK ARCHITECTS | 470 BROOME ST, 5TH FLOOR, SOUTH
NEW YORK, NEW YORK 10013 | T 212 274 9707 | F 212 274 9714
mpstudio@aol.com

MARPILLERO POLLAK was founded in 1998, after Linda Pollak and Sandro Marpillero worked on a number of design competitions together throughout the early to mid 1990s.

LINDA POLLAK teaches studios and seminars at the Harvard Graduate School of Design. She is co-author, with Anita Berrizbeitia, of *Inside Outside: Between Architecture and Landscape*, published in 1999 by Rockport Publications. For her research on urban landscape and outdoor space, she has received grants from the *National Endowment for the Arts*, the *Graham Foundation for Advanced Studies in the Fine Arts*, the *Wheelright Fellowship in Architecture*, and the *Milton Fund of Harvard University*. Pollak is Vice President of the Board of Directors of the *Storefront for Art and Architecture*, a member of the Board of Advisors of *Daidalos: Architecture, Art, Culture*, and Co-Editor of 9h Publications.

SANDRO MARPILLERO is an architect and public space artist, with offices in New York and Venice. Recent projects in addition to those with MP Architects include: the Hatta-Nagoya Elevated Train Stations in Japan; a house and grounds in Connecticut; and duplex apartments in the center of New York and Milan. He is Adjunct Associate Professor in the Urban Design Program at Columbia University, and also teaches at Princeton University and Harvard Graduate School of Design. He has taught design studios at the Institute of Venice, University of Virginia, University of Toronto, and Parsons School of Design. He is a member of the International Board of *Lotus International* and *Daidalos*, and a correspondent for *Casabella*.

SELECTED PROJECTS

Harlem RBI, Youth Baseball Park
East Harlem, New York City, NY, design 1999

Roy Wilkins Park
Outdoor classroom, stage & garden, Queens, New York City, NY, design 1999

Community Center Renovation & Addition
New York City Housing Authority, design 1998

Eib's Pond Park
Outdoor classroom, bridge, entrances, & docks, Staten Island, NY, design 1998–1999

National Art & Design Competition for Street Trees (CUNY)
First Prize Winner, competition 1998

Kidspace Child Development Center
"Children's Walk", House of Ruth, Washington, D.C., built 1999

Petrosino Park
Design competition, Storefront for Art and Architecture, New York City, NY, competition 1996–1997

Ecole Bilingue Expansion
Programming & planning study, (w/ Peter Tagiuri), Cambridge, MA, design 1995–1996

"Beyond the Box"
Design study of "big box" retail / Mid-Bronx Industrial District, New York City, NY, design 1995–1996

BCA Space, Boston Center for the Arts
First Prize Winner, Boston, MA, competition 1993

Olympic Garden for Atlanta
"Public Space in the New American City", Atlanta, GA, competition 1994

Building Public Space at Manhattan's Western Edge
Study of infrastructural and institutional scales, New York City, NY, design 1992

Urban Rooftop Garden
New York City, NY, built 1993

SELECTED BIBLIOGRAPHY

GAVIN KEENEY, "The Street Tree as Hunger Artist"
[National Art and Design Street Tree Competition review], Competitions (May 1999)

SANDRO MARPILLERO, "Strategic Thresholds"
Daidalos 71 (July 1999)

LINDA POLLAK, "Elevating Nature: The Roof Garden as Urban Retreat"
Domain (Fall 1998)

LINDA POLLAK, "Strategies for Building City Landscape"
Daidalos 73 (December 1999)

NINA RAPPAPORT, "Young Architects from New York"
Schweizer Ingenieur & Architekt (November 1997)

C. VOLKMAN AND LYNNETTE WIDDER, "Young Architects in New York"
Archis (Fall-Winter 1999)

LYNNETTE WIDDER, "in the Flatland"
Daidalos 63 (March 1997)

"Park for Boston's South End"
Oculus (1994)

"BCASpace: Gateway Project"
Harvard Architecture Review 11 (New York: Princeton Architectural Press, 1999)

"Eib's Pond Park"
Harvard Design Magazine (January 2000)

"Requalification of a Marginal Site in Manhattan"
[14th Street Pier], Casabella (January-February 1993)

26

DANADJIEVA & KOENIG – TIBURON

TOPOGRAPHIC TERRITORIES

Combining urban design, landscape architecture and architecture, Danadjieva and Koenig Associates have integrated into the design of public places modernist tectonic sensibilities and expressive readings of cultural context. The office focus on primarily large-scale facilities has yielded projects that rigorously and poetically integrate infrastructure and landscape. Many of these projects have an intense archaic essence that relates the urban condition back to the monumental cycles of the natural world.

Angela Danadjieva started her design career in Sofia, Bulgaria – as an architect – and she first worked in film production, in Sofia, as a set designer. Her work carries implicit traces of this early exposure to the cinematic experience of space. In California, she worked in association with Charles Moore and Lawrence Halprin – circa 1966, the time of the seminal Sea Ranch – in establishing an interdisciplinary approach to landscape architecture that is borne out over the years in projects that embrace theatricality and programmed movement through complex architectonic sequences. Plunging spaces, as with Moore, are part of Danadjieva's spatial vocabulary. Her work with Halprin in creating urban fountains, canyons and waterfalls is imbued with an appreciation of the sublime forces of natural topographic systems. Ira's Fountain in Portland, Oregon (1978) is indicative of this on-going exploration, in concrete- and gravity-based water systems, of extreme representations of architectonic sublimity.

26
Ira's Fountain, Seattle, WA, model view

27
Ira's Fountain, A.D. detail

28
Piggott Memorial Corridor, Seattle, WA, winter view

29
Piggott Memorial Corridor, spring view

27

28

29

An important urban landscape design element that returns in varied permutations in numerous Danadjieva and Koenig Associates' projects is the "bridging" typology. It serves as a means of restoring order to fragmented urban systems while purposely embracing the 'cinematic' experience of the city. Two related projects feature this element: The Piggott Memorial Corridor of 1984 in Seattle, Washington completes the link between downtown Seattle and the residential First Hill community first initiated in Danadjieva's Freeway Park a decade earlier. Freeway Park restored the primary linkage between two parts of the city severed by the 1960s construction of the Interstate-5 corridor. This was accomplished by re-claiming the air rights over the highway and by appropriating the rooftops of two nearby parking garages. Heavily planted, with a concrete gorge and waterfall, Freeway Park bridges the chasm between two at-grade pedestrian zones. Piggott Memorial Corridor closed the equation by connecting Freeway Park to University Street by way of a ramped bridge. The Corridor is animated by five fountains and a watercourse that flows through the concrete structure reappearing at folds along the horizontal slab. The concrete structure spans the deeply cut topography of the 1-acre site suggesting the topographic extremes of the Cascade Mountain range. It is both ramped and stepped to allow the handicapped through-passage.

24

31

32

30
Freeway Park, Seattle, WA, canyon

31
Freeway Park, bird's-eye view in autumn

32
Freeway Park, waterfall

33

34

This heightened sense of drama and scenic spectacle plays well in both urban and ex-urban environments. Danadjieva & Koenig's unbuilt Future Park is a 100 000-sq.-ft. enclosed educational and exhibition space based on the geometry of limestone geode crystals. Intended to complement the Indianapolis White River Park promenade, a linear park framed by 1300 limestone blocks with sculptural friezes of buildings constructed using Indiana limestone (including New York City's Empire State Building), the cultural facility would feature experimental virtual reality technologies and an IMAX cinema. The tinted glass panels of the faceted roof plane would be illuminated by day by the migration of the sun, east to west, and at night by a laser light show from within the crystalline structure of the building.

Danadjieva & Koenig's intense elaboration and amelioration of urban topography (natural and man-made) is an extreme act of making evident the lapsed interrelatedness of urban territories. The tectonic and superimposition of form upon form salvages the fragmentation of American cities through the strenuous recollection of adjacent but disjointed or unacknowledged sites.

33
White River Park Promenade, Indianapolis, IN, Rose Window

34
Future Park, pavilion, model

35

36

WASHINGTON STATE CONVENTION CENTER — SEATTLE WITH TRA ARCHITECTS

The Convention and Trade Center was built over the I-5 freeway and is contiguous with Danadjieva and Koenig's Freeway Park. The opportunity to add this layered glass, steel and concrete structure to the 1960s highway corridor further integrated the texture of the area. Working with TRA Architects, Danadjieva and Koenig's contribution transcended the design of exterior and interior gardens and influenced the form of the building itself. Responding to local opposition to the imposition of a high-profile box, the architects devised a scheme that would horizontally and vertically stratify the functions of the building and connect to DKA's earlier Freeway Park design. The city preferred a different location for the center but the freeway air rights site prevailed because of its proximity to downtown. Vehicular access and parking were stowed at the lowest levels with visitor facilities stacked overhead. North and south vehicular access is provided to diminish impact on surrounding streets. The glass fenestration was selected for its capacity to reflect the dramatic ambient atmospheric conditions of Seattle. The green spaces of the surrounding decks and terraces and the changing skies of Puget Sound impart to the glass an organic opacity.

The building envelope wraps 100 000 sq. ft. of exhibition space, 50 000 sq. ft. of meeting rooms, 20 000 sq. ft. of retail facilities and a majestic 30 000 sq. ft. lobby – all perched above the I-5 freeway. The surrounding park literally enters into the building at the lobby and galleria with vegetation, water and vertically stripped poured-concrete interior elevations echoing the exterior park water features and the distant Cascade Mountains.

The public spaces surrounding the convention center withstood – if not sponsored – the December 1999 demonstrations against the World Trade Organization when 85 000 environmentalists, anarchists and pacifists converged on Seattle. These generous spaces were later shut down, and subject to curfew, after federal marshals criticized the Seattle police for allowing the mostly peaceful demonstrators to block access to the convention center, stranding the international delegates in their hotel rooms.

35
Washington State Convention Center, Seattle, WA, interior lobby

36
Washington State Convention Center, bird's-eye view

WEST POINT WASTEWATER TREATMENT PLANT – SEATTLE

Danadjieva and Koenig Associates' environmental mitigation and design work for the West Point Wastewater Plant on Puget Sound included the overall site planning, visual and aesthetic considerations and design of supporting infrastructure. Yet perhaps it is the infrastructure that is most compelling. The sinuous strands of reinforced concrete weaving through the waterside site give the project a startling industrial edginess. The ribbons are spatially complex forms that shift and twist partly due to perspectival shifts in the approaches to the complex but otherwise as reflections of the layered, stepped geological strata of the site. They are empathetically related to the human body as sinews and arteries of the integral architectural systems.

By projecting the alluvial plain of the lower peninsula upwards, primarily to hide the main buildings, the industrial image of the project will in time soften as plants colonize and veil the 'bleached bones' of the access causeways, retaining walls and ramps. A major longitudinal cut into the hillside required the insertion of a 60-ft.-high retaining wall and detailed environmental impact studies to minimize changes to the hillside hydrological condition, safeguarding the coniferous forest above the wastewater plant. The naturalistic lake placed at the edge of the site, next to Puget Sound, is the collection basin for hillside water routed under the industrial facility.

The pedestrian zones alongside the water, planted with wildflowers and grasses – the supplemental mitigation zones – follow the contours of the low-lying land. The immensity of the plant facility – partly extant, partly new – disappears behind layers of vegetated infrastructure and the 180 000-cu.-yd. earth berm that wraps around the plant perimeter wall. Danadjieva and Koenig's concrete ribbon walls – though impressive from a purely aesthetic point of view – are the essential structural system holding both the earth berm and the upper hillside in place. The scrappier vegetation of both the real and instrumental elevated landscape will eventually produce a screen all but occluding the main block and twin-domed tanks of the wastewater filtration facility.

37
West Point Wastewater Treatment Center, Seattle, WA, bird's-eye view of Puget Sound

38
West Point Wastewater Treatment Center, plan

39
West Point Wastewater Treatment Center, ramp detail

37

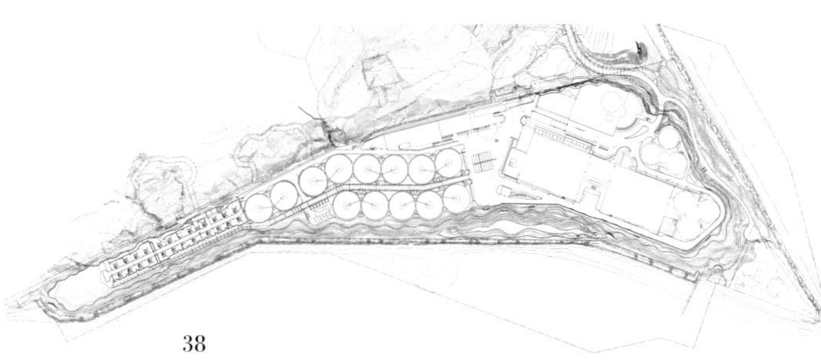

38

39

40

41

40
West Point Wastewater Treatment Center, Discovery Park lagoon

41
West Point Wastewater Treatment Center, wetlands sketch

THOMAS POLK PARK — CHARLOTTE

Thomas Polk Park represents one fourth of a proposed urban master plan for the historic heart of the central business district of Charlotte, North Carolina. The park itself is dwarfed by the surrounding office towers but establishes nonetheless a presence through a 24-ft.-high granite water feature and stone columns and groves at the outer edge. The remaining four corners of the carrefour are also to feature water utilized to symbolically represent 'historical ambiance' through metaphoric associations with the cultural history of the original Native American settlements of the region.

The water of the fountain, like medieval and baroque fountains of Europe, carries metaphorical content through both its route through the granite form and through its relative transparency as it passes over sculpted bas-relief tablets commemorating historic episodes in pre- and post-colonial Charlotte-Mecklenburg. The water is given added expressive potency through illumination that effectively transforms the positive form of the fountain into a twilit stage set. The underwater light sources provide an uncanny and preternatural aura to the water, which is used as a physical and metaphoric veil obscuring the bas-relief tablets and signifying by increased opacity a more distant and remote historicity. Blanks provide for the inscription of future histories.

The floor of the plaza and the outline of the fountain pools are conscious interpretations of Native American geometric figures, most notably the repeated chevron pattern evoking movement and the passage of time. The brick and granite floor pattern simultaneously is a choreographic score leading to and from the main entrance to the plaza.

The plaza serves the dual purpose of representing both nature and history in the city center while satisfying the more prosaic, low-level civic and commercial diversions of the local white-collar business community.

42

43

44

42
Thomas Polk Park,
Charlotte, NC,
night view of fountain

43
Thomas Polk Park,
aerial view

44
Thomas Polk Park,
aerial view of plaza

DANADJIEVA & KOENIG ASSOCIATES | P.O. BOX 939 | 1970 STRAITS VIEW DRIVE |
TIBURON, CA 94920 | T 415 435 2000 | F 415 435 0896
projects@dkassociates.com | www.dkassociates.com

DANADJIEVA & KOENIG is an architectural, landscape architectural and urban planning studio based in Tiburon, CA, in Marin County, north of downtown San Francisco.
ANGELA DANADJIEVA came to the United States from Sofia, Bulgaria after winning the International Design Competition for the San Francisco Civic Center Plaza in 1966. She is a graduate of the Architecture School at the State University in Sofia and further specialized in architecture at the Ecole Nationale Supérieure des Beaux Arts in Paris. Upon arrival in California, in 1966, Angela Danadjieva worked as project designer for landscape architect Lawrence Halprin on numerous urban design projects including Ira's Fountain in Portland, OR and Freeway Park in Seattle, WA. This association continued until 1976, with the founding of Danadjieva & Koenig Associates. Danadjieva is currently a member of the International Institute of Architects, the Urban Design Institute, and the American Planning Association.
DKA has received numerous awards for excellence in urban design and environmental remediation, foremost among these the accolades for the $578 million West Point Wastewater Treatment Plant on Puget Sound (1997), in Seattle, Washington.

SELECTED PROJECTS

West Point Wastewater Treatment Plant
Seattle, WA, built 1997

Future Park
Indianapolis, IN, design 1994

Thomas Polk Park
Charlotte, NC, built 1993

Freeway Park Expansion
Washington State Convention Center, Seattle, WA, built 1992

Discovery Park Bridge/Underpass
Seattle, WA, built 1992

Mission Bay Development Plan
San Francisco, CA, design 1988

Indiana White River State Park Promenade
Indianapolis, IN, built 1991

Freeway Park Expansion
Piggott Memorial Corridor, Seattle WA, built 1984

Freeway Air-Rights Development Masterplan
Freeway Park, Pigott Memorial Corridor, Washington State Convention and Trade Center, Seattle, WA, design 1983

Ira's Fountain
(w/ Lawrence Halprin and Associates), Portland, OR, built 1978

Freeway Park
(w/ Lawrence Halprin and Associates), Seattle, WA, built 1976

SELECTED BIBLIOGRAPHY

FRANCISCO ASENSIO CERVER (ED.), World of Environmental Design: Landscape Art
(Barcelona: Atrium, 1995)

ANGELA DANADJIEVA, "Envisioning the Future"
The Intimate Agenda: Inside the Creative Process
(Aspen: Third Eye Press, 1996)

ANDREA OPPENHEIMER DEAN, "Urban Camouflage"
Architecture (August 1990)

KIMBERLEY FISHER, "White River State Park – Indianapolis, Indiana"
Urban Land Institute (July-September 1992)

DOUGLAS GANTENBEIN, "West Point Sewage Treatment Plant - Seattle, Washington"
Architectural Record (August 1997)

ALEXANDER GARVIN AND GAYLE BERENS, Urban Parks and Open Space
(Washington: Urban Land Institute, 1997)

CHARLES LINN, "Focus On: Value-Added Infrastructure"
Architectural Record (June 1993)

STEVEN MANNHEIMER, "In Lapidary Limbo"
Landscape Architecture (January 1991)

DAVID PETERSEN, "Washington State Convention & Trade Center"
Urban Land Institute (April-June 1989)

KEVIN POWELL, "Topographic Statement"
Landscape Architecture (January 1992)

ROBERT RILEY, "Most Influential Landscapes"
Landscape Journal (Fall 1993)

PAUL ROBERTS, "Freeway Park: Still an Icon, But a Few Glitches"
Landscape Architecture (February 1993)

MELANIE SIMO, 100 Years of Landscape Architecture: Some Patterns of a Century
(Washington: ASLA Press, 1999)

ANDERSON & RAY – SEATTLE

HUMAN AND NATURAL DISCOURSE

Both continuous (integrated) and discontinuous (fragmented) systems mark the natural and the man-made worlds. The current appreciation of the disjointed or disjunctive is partly an outgrowth of both quantum physics and fractal geometry. Anderson & Ray exploit the cracks and fissures of this human and natural discourse – the discourse of nature is not mute but spoken in its own way in both form and disruption (force). The visitors center at Mount St. Helens National Volcanic Monument and Pritchard Beach Reserve, both in Washington State, are emblematic. Each of these projects is marked by natural and cultural disturbance – the so-called natural order (perceived and received) altered by unnatural and catastrophic events. In particular, Mount St. Helens erupted on May 18, 1980 leveling the surrounding forest, obliterating all infrastructures within 15 miles of the peak and leaving the once lush landscape a scorched wasteland.

The work of Anderson & Ray suggests new inroads to human observation and human interaction with environments beyond the everyday activities of human culture and an intense re-calibration of those at the heart of human inhabitation. Arthur Ross Terrace is an altogether different system than typically encountered in urban parks and plazas. Imbued with significance by the poetic-scientific *parti* of Kathryn Gustafson and the *de luxe* palette of natural and artificial materials (granite and fiber optics), it is likely to become a prime social venue for New Yorkers. Another project with Kathryn Gustafson – South Coast Plaza Strata Garden (2000) – carries multiple associations derived from regional plate tectonics, including a Mediterranean tranquility built up through a series of ramped and stepped planes, bubbling pools and shady Jacaranda groves. It is situated in a difficult location – a terrace overlooking a parking garage at an upscale shopping mall in Costa Mesa, California. These projects are artistic *études* – part provocation, part idealization. As public spaces, they function as places of repose and serenity. But they also have an implicit

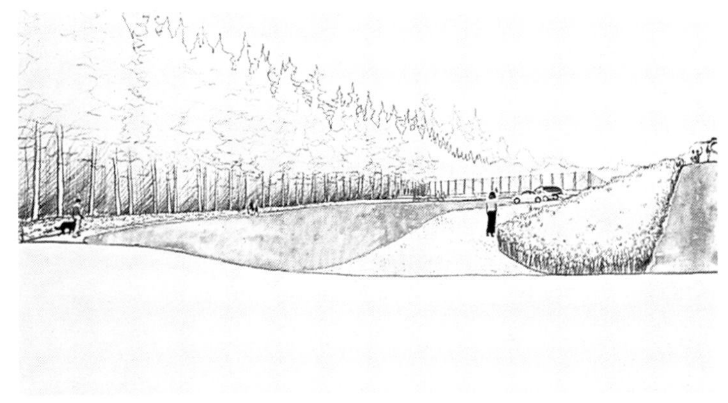

45

heuristic value – an educative edge – that belies their functional intention. At the site of Satsop Nuclear Garden (1995) the planned nuclear reactor was never fueled and the site is now to be redeveloped as a technology and business park. Its location on the Chehalis River, with access to Grays Harbor on the Pacific, makes its 400-acre site a potential recreational and commercial haven from the saturated environs of Seattle. The park, with its "Asphalt Sea" and "Salmon Hatchery / Cooling Tower", is pure ideology masked as amenity park.

Anderson & Ray characterize themselves as a "passionate" firm, "compelled by the challenge of creating places of utmost physical and ideological integrity". Their work exhibits not a romanticizing of natural orders, but a perhaps post-romantic realism given to rewriting and recoding fallen environments. This is especially evident in projects that are planned to evolve over long time frames. Fairweather Preserve in Medina, Washington (1999) – like Pritchard Beach – will require seasonal adjustments of the vegetation after an initial re-grading and installation of minimal amenities. This "landscape of perceived wildness and unpredictability" is sited on a 14-acre remnant of second-growth forest, alongside a congested freeway, and currently serves the nearby neighborhood as an active and passive recreational park. The principal design concept is to simply shape the naturally existing flora over many years to create reflective places with distinctive characteristics. The palette of materials summonsed to evoke tranquility or understanding – indeed to provoke contemplation – is drawn from the site's own integral physicality and facticity. Charles Anderson, descended from Indian blood, sees his projects from the perspective of the land and calls his work *kuwanlehlenta* – the Hopi word for 'to make beautiful surroundings'.

45
Fairweather Preserve,
Medina, WA,
entry perspective

SATSOP — NEAR ELMA WITH CNA ARCHITECTURE

On the Chehalis River, near Aberdeen, WA, the Satsop Nuclear Power Station has struck passersby – on the Olympic Loop Highway – as both absurd and sublime. Under construction since the 1970s, the 400-acre facility is a case study in unplanned obsolescence - it was never fueled. The Washington Public Power Supply System defaulted on $2.25 billion in municipal bonds in 1983 rendering the completion of the plant a moot point. In the early 1990s the site with its $2 billion worth of infrastructure was transferred to a local Public Development Authority. The vast site is under re-configuration as a technology and business park with recreational amenities.

The twin cooling towers, nearly 500 ft. high, are now slated to serve as amenity landscape. The immense interior clear spaces are large enough to house a football field, and, in a fascinating twist of fate, one will now shelter an arboretum - an elegant reflection of the surrounding forest.

In their masterplan, Anderson & Ray have been conjuring wry thematic forms of adaptive re-use since 1995 for this site. These phantasmatic forms include: Asphalt Sea, Salmon Hatchery / Cooling Tower and the arboretum. Having decided early on to retain the towers, Anderson & Ray, and the developers, have launched a high-profile demonstration of adaptive re-use for industrial facilities. The insertion of botanic collections and the transformation of unfinished portions of the energy plant to real and fictive environmental systems is a decisive convergence of iconic technological forms and the shifting shapes of nature.

With access to Grays Harbor, on the Pacific, the site may prove an irresistible destination for post-industrial tourism. The proximity to Seattle, with its turbo-charged economy, suggests that this patch of industrial wilderness may well embody the cybernetic dreamworld of the early information age - a fantasy summed up by the seminal Richard Brautigan poem *All Watched Over by Machines of Loving Grace* (c.1967). Salmon fishing in the Pacific Northwest will never be the same – Cyber-tech companies and blackmouth salmon now inhabit the same stretch of the imagination.

46
Satsop Nuclear Garden, near Elma, WA, aerial photograph of site

47
Satsop Nuclear Garden, plan

46

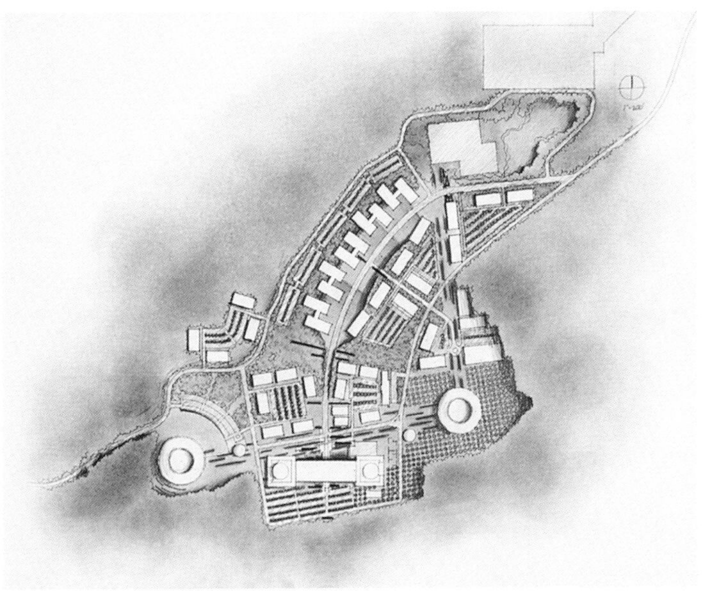

47

48

49

48
Satsop Nuclear Garden, cooling tower, photomontage

49
Satsop Nuclear Garden, cooling tower and sky

50

51

52

50
Satsop Nuclear Garden, cooling tower park with arboretum, plan

51
Satsop Nuclear Garden, observation tower

52
Satsop Nuclear Garden, perspective of promenade

PRITCHARD RESERVE – LAKE WASHINGTON

The notion of "alignment" carries multiple connotations – to straighten but also to correct or subjugate. To align nature (e.g. the parterre, bosque or canalized river) was part and parcel of past land-planning stratagems. Yet another meaning is to make connections. The 7-plus acre reserve at Pritchard Beach embraces this latter meaning as a type of integration or socialization not of the wild but with the wild. The shaping of the topography and the layout of paths and alternation of open and closed areas mimics the linguistic tools common to any speech act. These tools are means of naming and ordering – of making connections with the inchoate condition of first nature, an analogue for the 'preternatural' pre-linguistic state buried in language.

Anderson & Ray literally stage these alignments by first shaping the land (the phonetic contours) and adding the semantic markers (platforms, routes, amphitheater and geometric – logical and illogical – figures). This act of elevation to a higher perspective (viewpoint) is analogous to the principle of discourse within language itself. From the elevated platforms overviews (so-called meta-narratives) are possible that suggest the higher artistic and rational functions of language. The semi-natural features of the reserve are to be left to evolve with subtle input from the conservators of the site – alder groves will be encouraged (Alder Gallery) and a "Maple Cathedral" will be cultivated. Fantastic effects will be culled from the natural tableau – "Fairy Ring Matrix" and "Devil's Club Crescent" – by artistic suasion. This imposition of a cognitive template is a classic overlay technique, related in spirit to the 1970s McHargian landscape-planning methodology. But, here, Ian McHarg's implicit aversion to artifice (in *Design with Nature*, 1969) has metamorphosed (blossomed) into an affectionate humanistic reading of natural systems.

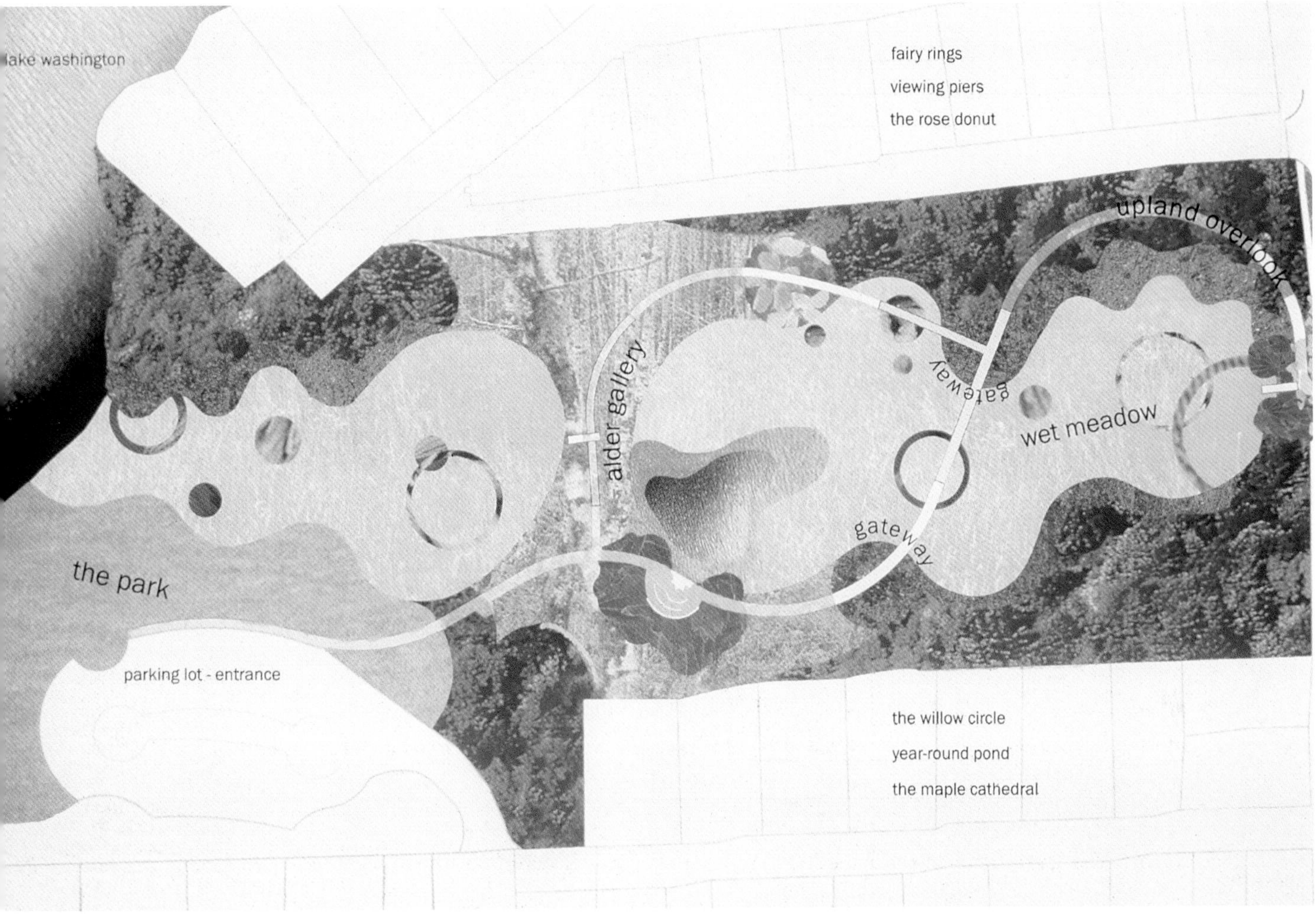

lake washington

fairy rings
viewing piers
the rose donut

upland overlook
alder gallery
gateway
wet meadow
gateway
the park
parking lot - entrance

the willow circle
year-round pond
the maple cathedral

53

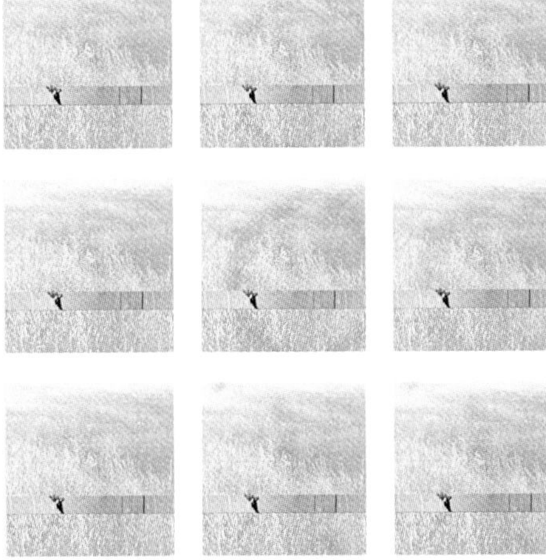

54

53
Pritchard Beach Reserve,
Lake Washington, WA,
plan

54
Pritchard Beach Reserve,
Fairy Ring Matrix

55 | 56

55
Pritchard Beach Reserve,
Maple Cathedral

56
Pritchard Beach Reserve,
bench detail
of Maple Cathedral,
photomontage

MOUNT ST. HELENS NATIONAL VOLCANIC MONUMENT – VANCOUVER, WASHINGTON WITH EDAW

After the 1980 catastrophic eruption of Mount St. Helens, a remote center was proposed to place visitors as close to the benighted site as possible. Visitor facilities for Mount St. Helens National Volcanic Monument in Washington State's Cascade Mountains were designed by Charles Anderson and Stephen Ray while both were working in the Seattle office of EDAW.

The main visitors center is located five miles from the volcanic crater and establishes observational and interpretive facilities within the Coldwater Lake Region of the Gifford Pinchot National Forest. In an effort to place visitors as close to the epicenter as possible Anderson and Ray sited the facility as a stage set within the deforested landscape on which the evolutionary and successional processes of the landscape are played out. As a laboratory, scientists are closely monitoring the site and studying the re-colonization of flora and fauna as well as the overall ecology of the blasted and denuded site.

The plan for the complex was established on an emotional foundation. Elements of the denuded site were retained and new elements mimicking the features of the blast zone were added as lyrical expressions of the aftermath of the May 18, 1980 eruption. Tapering lamp posts and fractured paving details suggest torched trees and broken earth. The planting plan specified only plants already growing in or native to the established boundaries of the park. On a master-planning level, the approach to the Center was conceived as analogous to the processional path through a cathedral: the approach road was interpreted as the "nave" and the architectural structure of the center as the "transept". The unapproachable volcanic crater was pictured as the "apse". The compensatory "journey" to the apse (crater) is strictly metaphorical. As in a cathedral, the journey is of a liminal order – the holy of holies is approachable only as a function (movement) within perception.

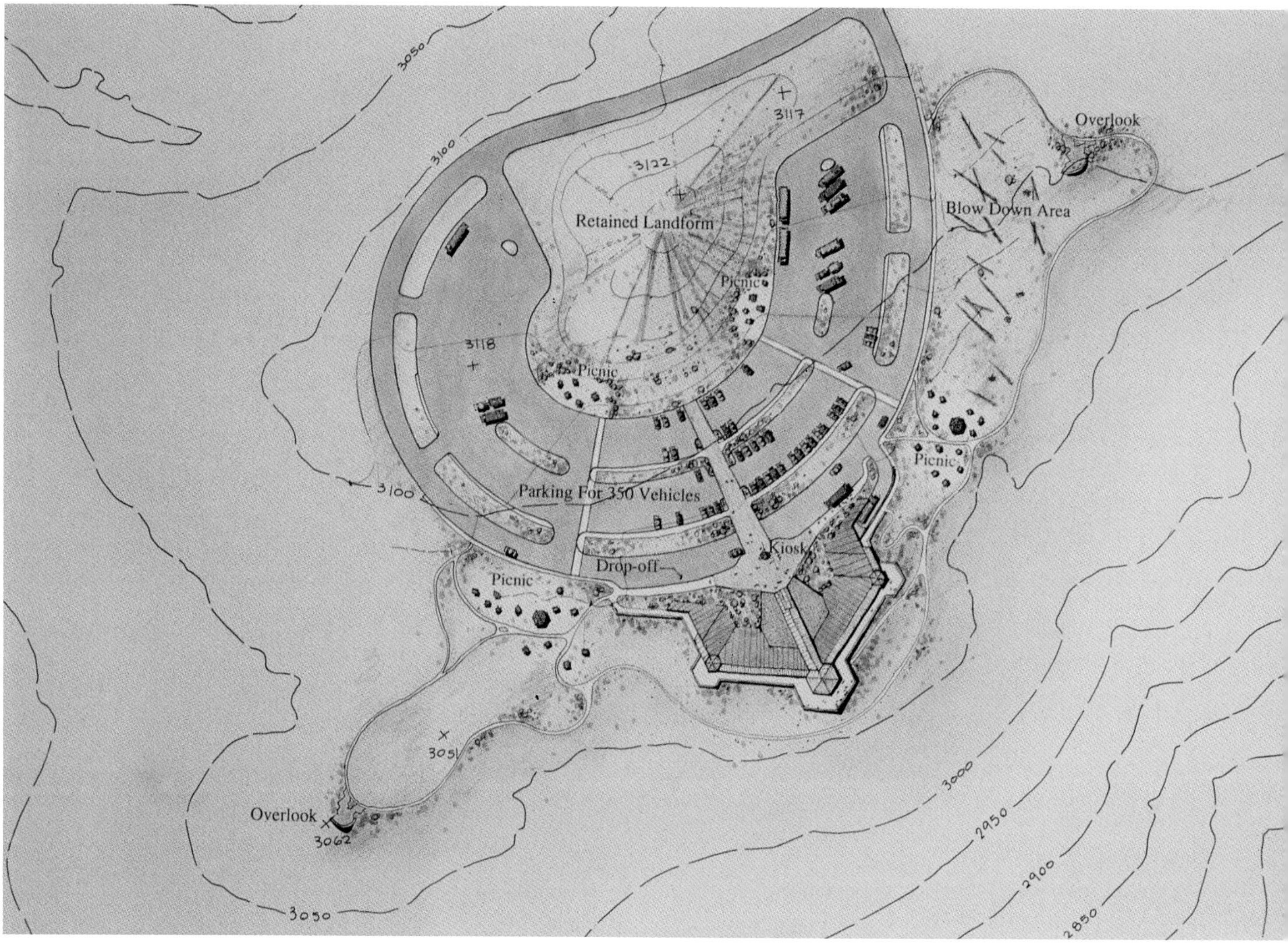

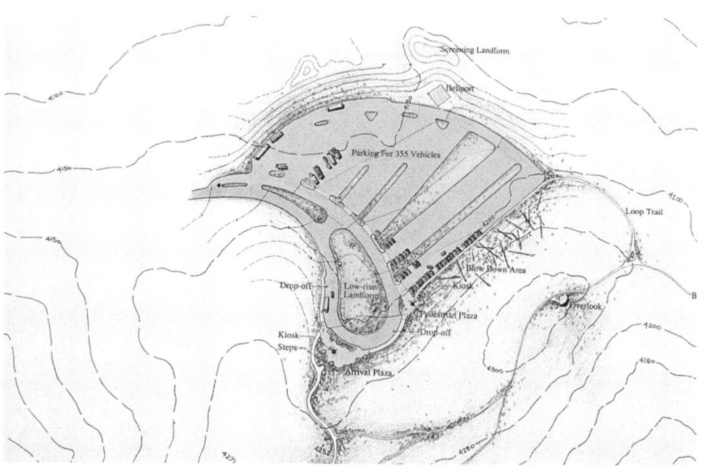

57|58

59

57
Mount St. Helens National Volcanic Monument, Vancouver, WA, Coldwater Lake Visitors Center, plan

58
Mount St. Helens National Volcanic Monument, Johnston Ridge Observatory, plan

59
Mount St. Helens National Volcanic Monument, Coldwater Lake Visitors Center, aerial view

60

61

ANDERSON & RAY | 811 FIRST AVENUE, SUITE 404 | SEATTLE, WASHINGTON 98104
T 206 264 9888 | F 206 264 1334
contact@anderson-ray.com | www.anderson-ray.com

ANDERSON & RAY is a studio of 12 people, including the two principals, Charles Anderson and Steve Ray. The studio is located in the Pioneer Square historic district of downtown Seattle. In recent years, they have enjoyed a strong working relationship with landscape designer Kathryn Gustafson.

CHARLES ANDERSON worked with numerous designers prior to establishing Anderson & Ray, including Richard Haag, James Turrell, Ron Wigginton, Peter Walker, Laurie Olin, and Ian McHarg. Stephen Ray worked for Richard Haag and EDAW.

CHARLES ANDERSON AND STEPHEN RAY'S collaborations in the Seattle office of EDAW, in particular the design and implementation of the Coldwater Lake Visitors Center and Johnston Ridge Observatory at the Mount St. Helens National Volcanic Monument in Washington State, led to the founding of their own firm in 1994.

SELECTED PROJECTS

Stadium, First & Goal and Public Stadium Authority
Seattle, WA, to be built 2002

Exhibition Center, First & Goal and Public Stadium Authority
Seattle, WA, to be built 2002

Bremerton Naval Hospital
Bremerton, WA, to be built 2002

South Coast Plaza
(w/ Kathryn Gustafson), Costa Mesa, CA, built 2000

Arthur Ross Terrace, American Museum of Natural History
(w/ Kathryn Gustafson), New York, NY, built 2000

Fairweather Preserve
Medina, CA, design 1999

Medina Creek
Medina, CA, design 1999

Roxhill Wetland, Department of Parks and Recreation
Seattle, WA, design 1999

Pritchard Beach Reserve, Department of Parks and Recreation
Seattle, WA, built 1999

Greg Davis Park, Department of Parks and Recreation
West Seattle, WA, built 1999

Colman Park
Seattle, WA, built 1999

Seward Park
Seattle, WA, built 1997

Hutchins Open Space, Department of Neighborhoods
Seattle, WA, built 1997

Coldwater Lake Visitors Center
Mount St. Helens (w/ EDAW), Vancouver, WA, built 1995

Johnston Ridge Observatory
Mount St. Helens (w/ EDAW), Vancouver, WA, built 1995

Satsop Nuclear Garden
Near Elma, WA, design 1995–2000

SELECTED BIBLIOGRAPHY

GAVIN KEENEY, "Seattle, Silos+Salmon: What to do About 'Whoops'"
Architectural Record (June 2000)

CHARLES ANDERSON, Native Plant Alliance: A Manual of Native Plant Communities
(Seattle: Cascade Biomes, 1995)

EVE M. KAHN, "Mount St. Helens: Super-Real Reclamation"
Landscape Architecture (February 1994)

MICHAEL LECCESE, "Volcanic Ventures"
Landscape Architecture (February 1993)

"Under the Volcano"
Landscape Architecture (June 1991)

60
Mount St. Helens National Volcanic Monument, Coldwater Lake Visitors Center, entrance

61
Mount St. Helens National Volcanic Monument, Johnston Ridge Observatory, model

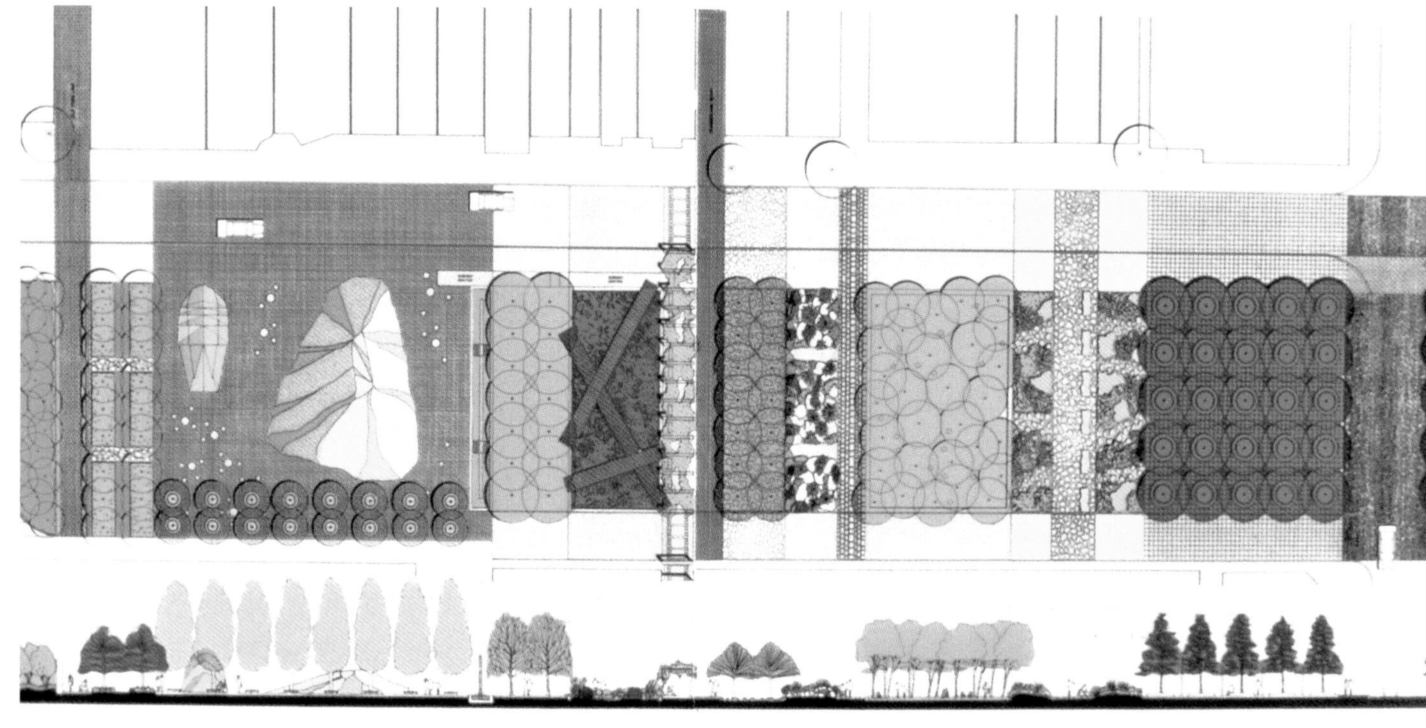

62

KEN SMITH LANDSCAPE ARCHITECT – NEW YORK

IDIOSYNCRATIC PUBLIC OPEN SPACE

Ken Smith Landscape Architect is a small interdisciplinary firm working primarily on urban design projects that address the conceptual and artistic aspects of public open space. These projects accept the existing infrastructure as the prevailing mode of organization within the city while attempting through analytical studies and site-specific proposals to alter that elemental level of experience and include highly integrated and diverse iterations of standard typologies – e.g. the plaza, the street, the garden and the park. It is also engaged in exploring more idiosyncratic contemporary types, such as the ubiquitous strip, 'leftover' land associated with modern infrastructure, or the temporary 'park', a device used for 'parking' land prior to wholesale re-development.

Recent innovations in sequencing urban landscape experience have led the studio in the direction of timed or syncopated landscape. This theory, partly derived from minimalist music, was applied to the San Francisco Light Rail Trackway Paving Study (1998–1999) in the form of details that

62
Yorkville Park, Toronto, Canada, plan/section

63
Yorkville Park, bird's-eye view

64
Yorkville Park, pergola

65
Yorkville Park, mist and illuminated columns

66
Yorkville Park, prairie and wood

63

64

65

66

incorporated timed sequences along the 5.5-mile stretch of urban rail. This concept of timed, sequential form returns in a perhaps ironic mode in the Merrick Boulevard Median Planting Study (1999), there applied through variations in the median planting.

Ken Smith's hyperborean Yorkville Park in Toronto, Ontario – a project realized while working with Martha Schwartz – is a figurative exploration of Victorian-Edwardian "collection boxes". The park, as a result, interacts with the surrounding period architecture in a purely symbolic-symbiotic manner. Subdivided into mini-parks, Yorkville Park collects elements of the Canadian landscape, including a large piece of the granite substrate underlying much of the Canadian wilderness. Marsh, prairie, and single-species groves of trees thematically orchestrate the horizontally and vertically layered, orthogonal site plan. The layering strategy is symptomatic of the context: the park is built over a subway station.

A fascinating contemporary tangent of environmental design is the phenomenon of purely temporary landscape – inclusive of gallery installations. An example is the Glowing Topiary Garden, which first appeared in 1997 in Liberty Plaza in downtown Manhattan, during the winter holiday season, and has since metamorphosed into small-scale reiterations inclusive of the installation of two cones in the 1999 Comité Colbert trade fair at Grand Central Terminal's Vanderbilt Hall in New York City. The recurring motif of topiary – albeit a non-reactionary and ironic take on the form – is used as a device for contingent renderings of spatial difference in otherwise predictable venues.

Ken Smith's streetscapes are based on a close reading of modernist urban landscape with a decidedly contemporary concern for texture and careful modulation of the characteristic strip typology. These projects involve minute analysis of paving details and street furnishings, often at full- or half-scale. The study of Pier A Plaza (1996), with Claire Weisz, and the Marginal Street Master Plan (1996), both for areas adjacent to Battery Park City, utilized landmark design methodologies – materials and gestures derived from historic New York districts. These projects, however, counter the backward looking typology of Battery Park City by relying instead on the essentialist and modernist appeal of integral formal logic *and* the quixotic post-cultural quest for radical contingency through animated, sensuously detailed and carefully calibrated programming and materiality.

67

68

69

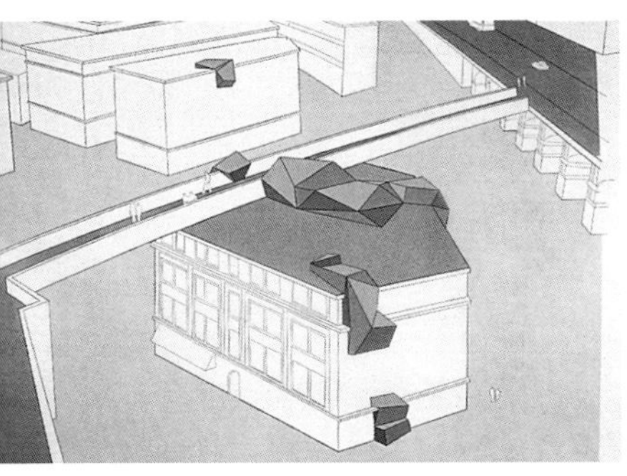

70

71

72

67
Pier A Plaza,
New York City, NY,
existing conditions,
aerial view

68
Pier A Plaza,
proposed plaza,
model view

69
Pier A Plaza,
planter/circular
bench model

70
Mutant Gardens,
Lausanne, Switzerland,
axonometric

71
Aluminum Garden,
New York City, NY,
upper terrace

72
Aluminum Garden,
view to lower terrace

73

73
MUNI Trackway Paving,
San Francisco, CA,
collage of paving pattern

The San Francisco MUNI trackway will thread through residential and commercial districts of the city serving as a commuter rail line within the larger public transit system of subways, ferries and buses. Ken Smith, as a member of the art team commissioned to study the aesthetic aspects of the rail corridor, defined the project in terms of drawing a "line in the landscape" that dramatizes the passage through the swelling topography of San Francisco. The concept draws on variations of color, texture and lighting to mark zones within the corridor with distinctive qualities already implicit in the route that traverses streets and causeways. The subdivisions within the trackway study are based on the existing spatial structure of the rail corridor and its strip morphology. The occurrence of platforms, straining poles for cables and lighting standards established the basic rhythmic order of the "timed" sections.

These time signatures relate to the speed of the train as it passes through multi- and single-use zones along the right of way. The pattern 'quickens' with the speed of the train. The "default" pattern representative of "whole time" (66–100 linear ft.), which occurs throughout the exclusive right of way, is comprised of alternating red and black concrete strips with the red portion carrying the rows of low-profile bot dots to discourage vehicles from entering the rail trackway. "Quarter time" (15–20 linear ft.) paving occurs at mixed-flow sectors of the corridor and does not include the speed bumps, since crossing traffic utilizes the right of way. Median plantings are used to direct and control these more complex zones. "Triple time" (28–32 linear ft.) paving is employed between the two other sections and implies a more rapid passage through areas free of cross traffic. The chief concern of the proposal is to provide 'identity' to the trackway through delineation of pedestrian and non-pedestrian areas, vehicular and non-vehicular lanes and 'gray' or hazard zones. The main device for marking these zones is the bot dot or speed bump, a cast concrete tile applied to the surface of the right of way, and the "rumble strip" or scored sections of concrete that work both visually and aurally. Passing cars will vibrate and 'sound' the passage when crossing the scored section of roadbed. The 'signing' and 'singing' of these variable systems is carried in the wide array of surfacing options. Tinted concrete, speed bumps, rumble strips and imbedded reflective particles will guide vehicles and pedestrians through the MUNI system that operates out of necessity at grade, integrated with the urban streetscape. The paving system recalls French New Wave filmmaker Jean-Luc Godard's maxim that film is "truth at 24 frames per second".

74

75

The Merrick Boulevard Median Planting Study recapitulates much of this theoretical paradigm in a more constrained venue – the concrete reinforced traffic island of urban streets often designated after the fact as ‘landscape’. The 7-block, mile-long section of this Queens *via media* is delineated in the plan by plantings that represent the typical vehicular speed of 30 miles per hour or 45 ft. per second. A notorious drag-racing strip at nighttime, the more aggressive drivers will merely experience a revved-up version of the landscape collage caught in the speeding beam of their headlights. The rugged planting palette is an admixture or a synoptic overview of plant materials typically found in extant Queens gardens – hydrangeas, spireas, daylilies, roses – and the classic English cottage garden style of Gertrude Jekyll that relies on masses of shrubs to provide “bones” for a garden of ‘hearty’ perennials. The median strip as English cottage garden is an appropriate analog for present-day Queens, which started life as a garden city refuge for harried Manhattanites.

74
MUNI Trackway Paving,
collage at drawbridge

75
MUNI Trackway Paving,
collage of signage

76

77

78

MALCOLM X PLAZA — NEW YORK CITY

Malcolm X Plaza is a culturally politicized enhancement of a Harlem district just north of Central Park. Ken Smith, with architect Zevilla Jackson-Preston, developed the design as a means of giving specific character to the intersection of St. Nicholas Avenue and Malcolm X Boulevard while honoring Malcolm X, the assassinated leader of the American Black Muslim movement. The plaza, over a subway station, draws on traditional Islamic-Persian motifs – in particular the Charhar-Bagh typology, with its integration of sacred geometric forms and crisscrossing diagonals. The plaza becomes, as a result, a garden or grove with its dominant sight lines aligned with the existing avenues. A 30-60-90 degree triangular form is repeated throughout the design in three- and two-dimensional structural and decorative aspects.

The plaza is paved in a carpet pattern with earth tones of brown, black, tan, terracotta and slate green. Plant groups are stylized versions of traditional garden schemes with a Catalpa bosque superstructure. The shrub and perennial plantings include roses, as a mnemonic visual and olfactory reference to Persian gardens, and sturdy herbaceous species with an emphasis on yellow, white and cream-colored species. The flowering sequence begins around May 19, the birthday of Malcolm X.

76
*Malcolm X Plaza,
Harlem, New York City, NY,
proposed plaza,
model*

77
*Malcolm X Plaza,
planter/bench/paving,
model*

78
*Malcolm X Plaza,
paving detail,
model*

NEO-UTOPIAN TOPIARY

Tim Burton's bizarre film *Edward Scissorhands* (1990) notwithstanding, topiary has seen too few recent manifestations of its radical chic potential. To the late-modernist eye, today, new garden topiary is a mostly reactionary shortcut to status by the *nouveaux riches* – a garden-architectural throwback to another era. To the less ideologically inclined, it is often an elemental focal point for ironic post-modern posturing. A third possibility for topiary form, one that redeems highly sculpted plant forms as art, is to exploit the essence of the type for neo-utopian ends.

The Glowing Topiary Garden is a collaborative project by Ken Smith and Jim Conti, a lighting designer. The proposed 540-ft. linear re-deployment at the World Trade Center, for Battery Park City (1998), would have lined Church Street, at Christmastime, with 8 cones illumined with red and green light from within. The original sound installation from Liberty Plaza would have been re-calibrated to produce a greater sonic impact on the highly trafficked route through New York's Financial District – an event that would have established the migratory credentials of the project and underscored the transient nature of most urban landscape forms. This potential for enhancing urban public space with temporary garden installations has recently regained critical public acceptance with the urban installations by Christo and the proliferation of urban garden festivals, from London's yearly Chelsea Flower Show to the less frequent Lausanne Garden Festival.

Hair Gardens similarly appropriated the theme of topiary but as a methodology for sculpting body hair. The gallery installation at Max Fish, a SoHo bar, presented collaged images of couture models sprouting topiary-inspired hairstyles in a patently absurd and ironic homage to the style-conscious set that frequents New York's SoHo district. It suggested a variety of ways to hypothetically get a leg up on your fashionable friends through provocatively twisting and trimming body hair into garden forms – for example "Ear Hair Rockery" and "Chest Hair Maze". Through a series of photomontages using images from fashion magazines, Hair Gardens was pure and puerile provocation.

79
Liberty Plaza,
New York City, NY,
night view

80
Liberty Plaza,
nighttime axial view

81
Liberty Plaza,
nighttime with silhouettes

82
Comité Colbert,
New York City, NY,
Vanderbilt Hall,
Grand Central Terminal

79

80

81

82

83

84

An upstate New York residence, a 'Tudor style' suburban home, also received topiary treatment through a row of monumental topiary yews with peacock "finials". The modest house was pictured as a mock mansion through this tectonic gesture deliberately placed in the front garden as public spectacle.

These are not attempts to mimic or reference the great estates of past centuries. While nominally ironic, all three are serious formal innovations, given their quixotic design intentions. Whether Wall Street parking lot, East SoHo bar or Westchester suburban front yard – each project suits its respective location by classic modern dissociation. The quest for this critical aesthetic distance is the hallmark of neo-utopian impulses. And so, when the French luxury goods consortium Comité Colbert came calling, in 1999, how could one refuse?

83
Hair Gardens,
Max Fish Gallery,
New York City, NY,
Bouffant Topiary,
photomontage

84
Hair Gardens
Chest Hair Maze,
photomontage

KEN SMITH LANDSCAPE ARCHITECT | 79 CHAMBERS STREET | NEW YORK, NY 10007
T+F 212 791 3595
ksla@earthlink.com

KSLA is a 3-person studio in Manhattan, New York City primarily practicing in the public realm. Employing a modernist sensibility with late-modern notions of complexity and cultural identity, the studio is concerned with identifying latent urban landscape and reformulating the pretext of these diverse spaces to include conceptual, historical and horticultural significance. The hybrid nature of these interventions introduces rich typological texture to public open space with human scale denoted in custom-crafted site details. In the mid 1990s, Ken Smith conducted a survey of modernist landscape in New York City and has advocated, through lectures and articles, the preservation and restoration of these significant gardens and plazas. He is a board member of the Architectural League of New York, a design critic at the Harvard University Graduate School of Design and an adjunct professor in the Urban Landscape Architecture Program at the City College of New York. Prior to establishing KSLA in 1992, Ken Smith worked in the New York and San Francisco offices of Peter Walker and Martha Schwartz, from 1986–1989, and was a partner in the San Francisco office of Schwartz Smith Meyer, from 1990–1992. He graduated from the Harvard University Graduate School of Design in 1986.

SELECTED PROJECTS

Third Street Light Rail, Muni Line
(w/ Bill and Mary Buchen and Chris Andrews), San Francisco, CA, to be built 2003

Hotel Garden Room
(Nest Magazine), Room 401, Roger Smith Hotel, New York City, NY, installation 2000

Lever House Restoration
(w/ Landscape Agency New York), New York City, NY, to be built 2000

Malcolm X Plaza
(Cityscape Institute w/ Hardy Holtzman Pfeiffer Architects, Cline Bettridge Bernstein, Anthony Williams and Roger Whitehouse and JP Design Group), New York City, NY, under construction 2000

HELP USA Children's Garden
under construction 2000

Science Museum of Virginia
Richmond, VA, to be built 2000

Mutant Gardens
(w/ Landscape Agency New York), Lausanne, Switzerland, design 1999

Aluminum Garden
New York City, NY, built 1999

Comité Colbert Garden Courtyard
(w/ Jim Conti), Vanderbilt Hall, Grand Central Terminal, New York City, NY, built 1999

110th Street & Harlem Gateway
(Cityscape Institute w/ Hardy Holtzman Pfeiffer Architects, Cline Bettridge Bernstein, Anthony Williams and Roger Whitehouse and JP Design Group), New York City, NY, design 1998

Hair Gardens, Max Fish Gallery
New York City, NY, exhibition 1998

Glowing Topiary Garden
(w/ Jim Conti), New York City, NY, built 1997

Pier A Plaza
(w/ Claire Weisz Architect and Design Writing Research), New York City, NY, design 1996

Marginal Street Linear Park
(w/ Claire Weisz Architect, Ohlhausen and Dubois Architects and Sam Schwartz Co.), New York City, NY, design 1996

Yorkville Park
(w/ Schwartz Smith Meyer Inc.), Yorkville, Ontario, built 1991

SELECTED BIBLIOGRAPHY

KOJI AIKAWA (ED.), "Linkages with Urban Activity"
Space Design (June 1998)

NILS BALLHAUSEN, "Aluminum Garden in New York"
Bauwelt (October 1999)

PAUL BENNETT, "Reinventing Harlem"
Landscape Architecture (June 1988)

FRANCISCO ASENSIO CERVER (ED.), MOISÉS PUENTE RODRIGUEZ (TEXT), Landscape Architecture 02
(Barcelona: Atrium, 1997)

GINA CRANDELL AND HEIDI LANDECKER (ED.), Designed Landscape Forum 1
(Washington: Spacemaker Press, 1998)

ROBERTA BRANDES GRATZ, "Filling the Void in Public Works"
Progressive Architecture (March 1995)

CATHERINE SLESSOR, "Delights"
Architectural Review (December 1998)

KEN SMITH, "Linear Landscapes"
Harvard Design Magazine (Spring 1999)

KEN SMITH, "Case Study: Preserving Dan Kiley's Work at Lincoln Center for the Performing Arts"
Preserving Modern Landscape Architecture, Proceedings of the Wave Hill Conference, ED. Charles Birnbaum (Washington: Spacemaker Press, 1999)

J. WILLIAM THOMPSON, "Excavating the Commonplace"
Landscape Architecture (December 1994)

"Landscape Creation Today"
[Profiles], Space Design (June 1998)

"Portfolios"
[Drawings by Landscape Architects], Landscape Architecture (May 1993)

IMMANENCE AND MODERNITY

Oslund & Associates practice landscape architecture in America's heartland – a conscious decision taken in homage to the vast open spaces of the Midwest. The prime motivation for designing within this milieu is the "power of the horizon" – the objectification of the relationship between the prairie and the sky. Their fascination with the horizon focuses in systems of horizontal expression – serial extension – that draw on the antecedents of the vernacular landscape and the aesthetics of modernist landscape. Employing the power of abstraction to emphasize the horizontal tableau of the Midwest plains, the studio is also concerned with encoding cultural memory and significance to overcome the aesthetic "disinterestedness" associated with art for art's sake. A tactile approach to detailing and interpretive approaches to native plant communities places their work outside the purely conceptual space of land art although periodic gallery installations explore the purely polemic nature of landscape vocabularies. Sod Suit and Missing Link are such hyperbolic expressions of landscape strophes. They attest to the re-occurrence of hyperbolic representations of the American lawn vis-à-vis the prairie.

These philosophical and aesthetic precepts are expressed at various scales and often utilizing unexpected materials, the latter typified by the institutional General Mills Courtyard (1995). The General Mills Courtyard is a glass-covered idyll with granite plinths set into a polished flagstone floor. The plinths support bare-naked expressions of terrestrial ecology in the form of a water table, a conical, vine-covered trellis and a somewhat 'archaic' freestanding bamboo and granite 'outcropping'. Patent Garden for Medtronic Corporation (1998), a biomedical engineering company, departs from contingent expressions of the local culture and celebrates the culture of a company with over 3 000 patents for various devices associated with medical science. The garden is a 100-ft.-by-100-ft. square with a tapered cor-ten steel wall that encloses a 75-ft.-diameter lawn and is inscribed with the numbers of Medtronic patents. A single maple tree provides 'human' scale.

The American heartland is a metaphoric rite of passage in the historical and political economies of the Country's self-image. This naïve sense of openness and innocence is countered in Oslund & Associates projects with a critical evaluation of its more complex and 'actual' culture.

85
The Missing Link, Minneapolis, MN, stacked sod fairway

86
Sod Suit, Harvard Graduate School of Design, Cambridge, MA, ready-to-wear

85

86

87

88

89

90

91

92

87
General Mills Courtyard, Golden Valley, MN, black granite water table

88
General Mills Courtyard, water table, granite slab and conical trellis

89
Modular Garden, Here, Here Gallery, Cleveland, OH, sand, tree, trough

90
Modular Garden, sand, root ball, trough

91
Patent Garden, Medtronic World Corporate Headquarters, Minneapolis, MN, bird's-eye view of model

92
Patent Garden, schematic model

93

WATER GARDEN – APPLETON WITH TALIESEN ARCHITECTS

Water Garden – a component within Wisconsin's Appleton Memorial Park and Arboretum – is a series of linked strips of water set into the slope of a hill and merging with the surroundings. The water emerges – fountain wall within – from beneath the pavilion (education center, offices) and flows through the artificial pools to spill into an aquatic 'natural' lake 7 ft. below the topmost elevation. The intermediate water terraces drop in 1-ft. increments over a 62-ft. expanse.

The master plan for the public facility, superimposed on paper company territory, is a guilt complex incarnate. The 70 acres, with cross-representational forms mirroring major ecosystems of the state, undertaken with Taliesen Architects, utilizes raised pathways – a methodology for traversing 'sacred' landscape – and mimics the 'forced march' of the contemporary art gallery. The subversive typology, funded by the affluent heirs to paper company fortunes, is supported by 6-ft.-wide axial boardwalks – referencing the Jeffersonian grid that was used to subdivide the virgin American wilderness into manageable sectors – 18 in. above grade. The Japanese tradition of maintaining critical distance from which to perceive landscape is also invoked.

The modest overall area of the Water Garden is provided additional depth, gravity and scale by the implantation of arcs of larch trees along the grass terraces between the watercourses. A boardwalk crosses the marsh zone that mediates between the formal apparatus of the terraces and the naturalistic zone beyond the garden.

93
Water Garden, Appleton, WI, model view

94

95

MARINE EDUCATION CENTER – APPLE VALLEY WITH HGA ARCHITECTS

Beneath the whale-back arris of the aquarium building and approached through an abstract estuarine landscape, the Marine Education Center stretches the limits of the imagination and begs the question "Why place a shark and dolphin tank in Minnesota?". A project with HGA Architects (Minneapolis), the central feature of the 40 000-sq.-ft. facility is a saltwater tank with oceanic systems. The garden entrance, in turn, makes the necessary connections between Minnesota, the Great Lakes and the Gulf of Mexico through miniaturized depictions of geological, hydrological and cultural links.

The procession of water to the sea is the organizing principle of the garden. The water, collected from the roof of the aquarium, passes through a galvanized steel pipe entering the garden through a suspended, perforated granite shield that produces a shower. The captured rainwater is then channeled into the garden through a series of sluices. Rocks collected from Lake Superior line the first 'naturalistic' sluice, which resembles a glacial outflow. The water flows next into a more formal 'canal' filled with rock-impressed cast-iron tiles alluding to the iron ore traditionally transported across the Great Lakes. Blocks of Mississippi granite are casually spread across the garden plaza as informal resting spots. A stainless steel bridge, flush with the plaza floor but passing over the recessed canal leads to the entrance of the aquarium.

94
Marine Education Center, Apple Valley, MN, model of aquarium and garden

95
Marine Education Center, model of bridge and watercourse

96
Marine Education Center, roof arris and entrance

97
Marine Education Center, canal and bridge

96

97

98
Marine Education Center, cast-iron canal

64

99

100

101

DAHL HOUSE, D.O.R. PLAZA — ST. PAUL WITH MARY MISS

The garden-architectural elements of the D.O.R. plaza were originally to be constructed from the remains of a small c.1858 house on the site of the proposed office complex. The building was to be moved 90 ft. and stripped of its spatial and physical contents. These, in turn, were to be spread over the site as a memorial to the former, modest residential unit. The controversial plan was not installed when it became clear that it was an implicit criticism of the very nature of taxation.

The domestic nature of the building was perceived as a notable counterpoint to the institutional anonymity of the Department of Revenue. By deconstructing the house, elements of its interior were to be replicated at various scales in the surrounding plaza. The foundation – limestone blocks – would be assembled as an outdoor room with terrazzo paving. The wood frame of the structure's roof would be copied as a freestanding pavilion also with terrazzo paving and seating elements of stainless steel wire mesh added. The interior spaces of the original 23-ft.-by-30-ft. house would be represented by wire mesh over a steel frame with the southern corner glazed for a cold weather shelter. The addition of brick-paved walkways, hedges, picket fencing and street trees complete the dissection of the house and its reconfiguration as a public garden. The bilateral symmetry of the plan supports the stripping concept and the proposal resembles an exploded isometric drawing or study of the all-American single-family house (home), albeit blown apart by the sheer force of the neighboring entity.

99
D.O.R. Plaza, St. Paul, MN, model view of platform

100 | 101 | 102
D.O.R. Plaza, bird's-eye model views

102

OSLUND & ASSOCIATES | 115 WASHINGTON AVENUE NORTH | MINNEAPOLIS, MN 55401
T 612 359 9144 | F 612 359 9625

OSLUND AND ASSOCIATES was established in 1998 in the historic warehouse district of Minneapolis as an intentionally modest landscape planning and design studio. The office is comprised of 5–6 persons and engages selectively in projects that have potential for embodying the firm's philosophy of place.
TOM OSLUND worked with Minneapolis architects Hammel Green and Abrahamson throughout the 1990s, on large corporate and civic planning projects, prior to creating Oslund & Associates. He received the Rome Prize Fellowship from the American Academy in Rome in 1991.
The firm's philosophy of place is based on an interpretation of the ecological and cultural framework of the American Midwest. The prairie, as a voluble signifier, influences most of Oslund & Associates' projects through its presence in the landscape as a great "field of dreams". Diminutive forms of lawn and prairie haunt the design of place, taking shape in forms as diverse as Sod Suit and Missing Links.
Installation art complements the production of the studio, primarily as a means of exploring new conceptual ground and re-visiting traditional landscape typologies.

SELECTED PROJECTS

Minnesota Orchestral Association Outdoor Performing Arts Center
(w/ HGA, Hodgetts & Fung), Minneapolis, MN, design 2000

Water Garden, Appleton Memorial Park and Arboretum
Appleton, WI, design 1996

Patent Garden, Medtronic Corporation
Minneapolis, MN, design 1998

General Mills Courtyard
Golden Valley, MN, built 1995

Marine Education Center
(w/ Hammel Green & Abrahamson Architects), Minnesota Zoological Garden, Apple Valley, MN, built 1998

Dahl House, D.O.R Plaza
(w/ Mary Miss), St. Paul, MN, design 1998

Modular Restorative Garden
Here, Here Gallery, Cleveland, OH, installation 1999

Weesner Family Amphitheater
Apple Valley, MN, c. 1993

Valparasio University Master Plan
Valparasio, IN, c. 1993

Missing Link
Minneapolis, MN, installation, c. 1990

Sod Suit
Cambridge, MA, installation, c. 1989

SELECTED BIBLIOGRAPHY

KATE CHRISTIANSON, "Garden Abstracts"
Metropolis (October 1993)

GUY COOPER AND GORDON TAYLOR, Paradise Transformed: The Private Garden for the 21st Century
(New York: Monacelli Press, 1997)

DEBORAH KARASOV AND STEVE WARYAN, Once and Future Park
(New York: Princeton Architectural Press, 1993)

TOM OSLUND, "Rome Prize Drawings"
Landscape Architecture (April 1993)

MARC PALLY, "Conceiving a Courtyard"
[Pasadena Police Building Public Art Competition], Places (Spring 1990)

CHERYL WEBER, "Articulating Winter"
Garden Design (Autumn 1990)

"Portfolios"
[Drawings by Landscape Architects], Landscape Architecture (May 1993)

"Landscape Creation Today"
[Profiles], Space Design (June 1998)

"Avant Gardeners"
[Profiles], Landscape Architecture (February 1990)

"Weesner Family Amphitheater"
International Design Magazine (July-August, 1993)

'ALL-AT-ONCE' URBANISM

The inspired urbanity of Michael Sorkin Studio might seem in passing to be a series of snapshots of incidental urbanism – "Architecture is a useful coincidence of form and life" (*Michael Sorkin Studio: Wiggle*, 1998) – but its principles are consciously conceived and broadly applied. Instead of anti-utopian dysfunctionalism and *La Jetée*-inspired anti-aestheticism typified by sci-fi and film noir urbanism, the so-called "low budget mysticism" favored by minimalist artists in the 1960s, the studio proposes cities of lyric organicity and shimmering eclecticism that resist structural fixity. This urban design methodology updates the values of the Enlightenment *weltanschauung* while prefiguring the build-out of post-industrial cities worldwide.

Imagining an all-encompassing elemental architecture with fluid boundaries, Sorkin Studio envisions cities with plastic, hybrid forms that induce appetites of "desirability". Picturing cities of closely connected tissues and often voluble, strutting signifiers, denoting an inexorable physicality, the cellular images are not collage cities or abstract and superhuman-scale interventions. Sorkin's idea of the city is fundamentally opposed to abstract dematerializations of landscape associated with normative urban planning, with implicit *de facto* mapping strategies and sublimation of capital flows often defined by the 'redlining' of ethnic, political and economic backwaters. Past urban planning models were an always re-programmable methodology underwritten by abstract forces all too often prodigiously anti-human and representing a surreptitious reduction of landscape to commerce.

In essence, post-cultural urbanism is an intricate tableau of elastic socio-political ideologies. Sorkin Studio works at a scale typically associated with master planning but denies the model the usual functional payload – zoned, typecast and intentionally sanitized readings of cultural diversity and the attendant aestheticized suppression of its outcome, structural anomie. Difference and anomie are recognized instead as protean factors of urban speciation – they are elective versus imposed. The social Darwinist aspects of modern municipal urban planning is inverted and a frenetic mosaic of floating architectural signs, infiltrated by parks and water (green and blue space), lifted and recessed strata, channeled and liberated transport, emphatic and coy services and anti-monumental and ironic-monumental 'stations of the cross', emerge. The implied 'crucified' subject – livable, public-spirited urbanism – is resurrected in a vision of full-blooded and full-figured urbanism.

103 | 104 | 105 | 106
Floating Islands, Hamburg, Germany, bird's-eye and perspective drawings

107
Brooklyn Waterfront, New York City, NY, perspective drawing

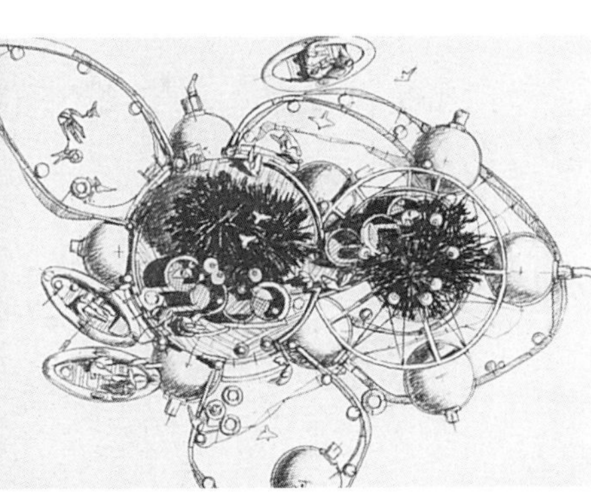

103 | 104

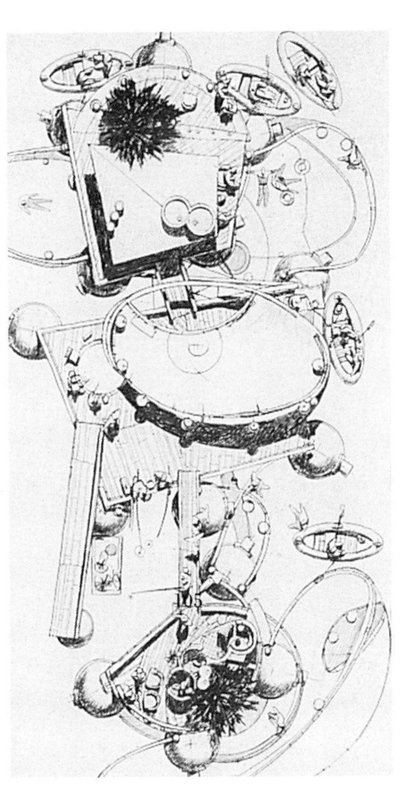

105

106

107

108

109

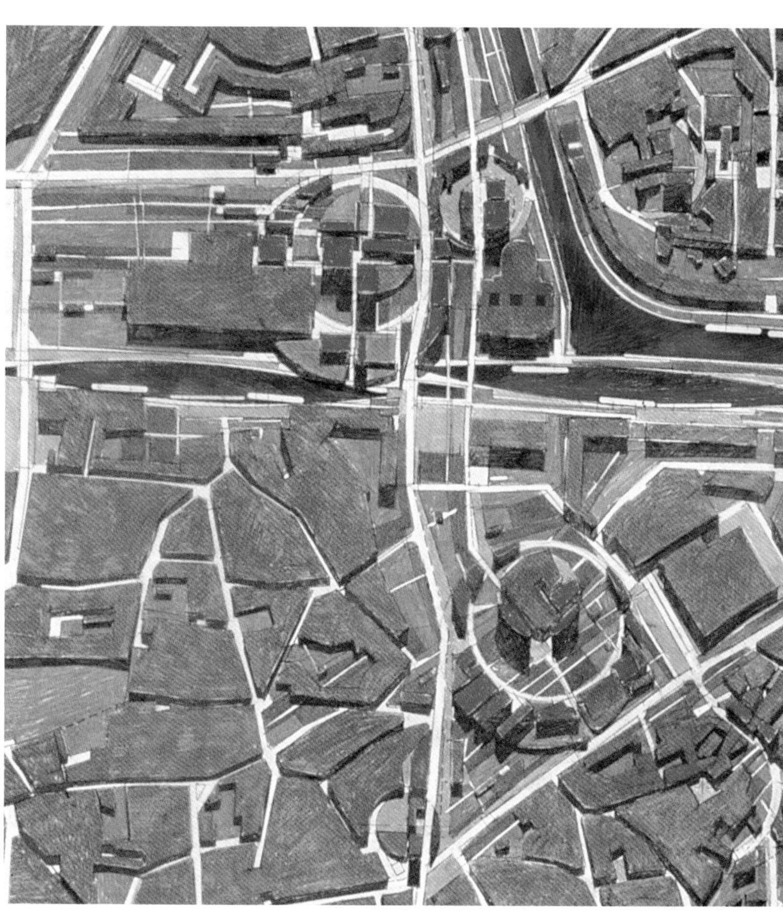

111

108 | 109
Black Triangle,
Leipzig, Germany,
perspective drawings

110

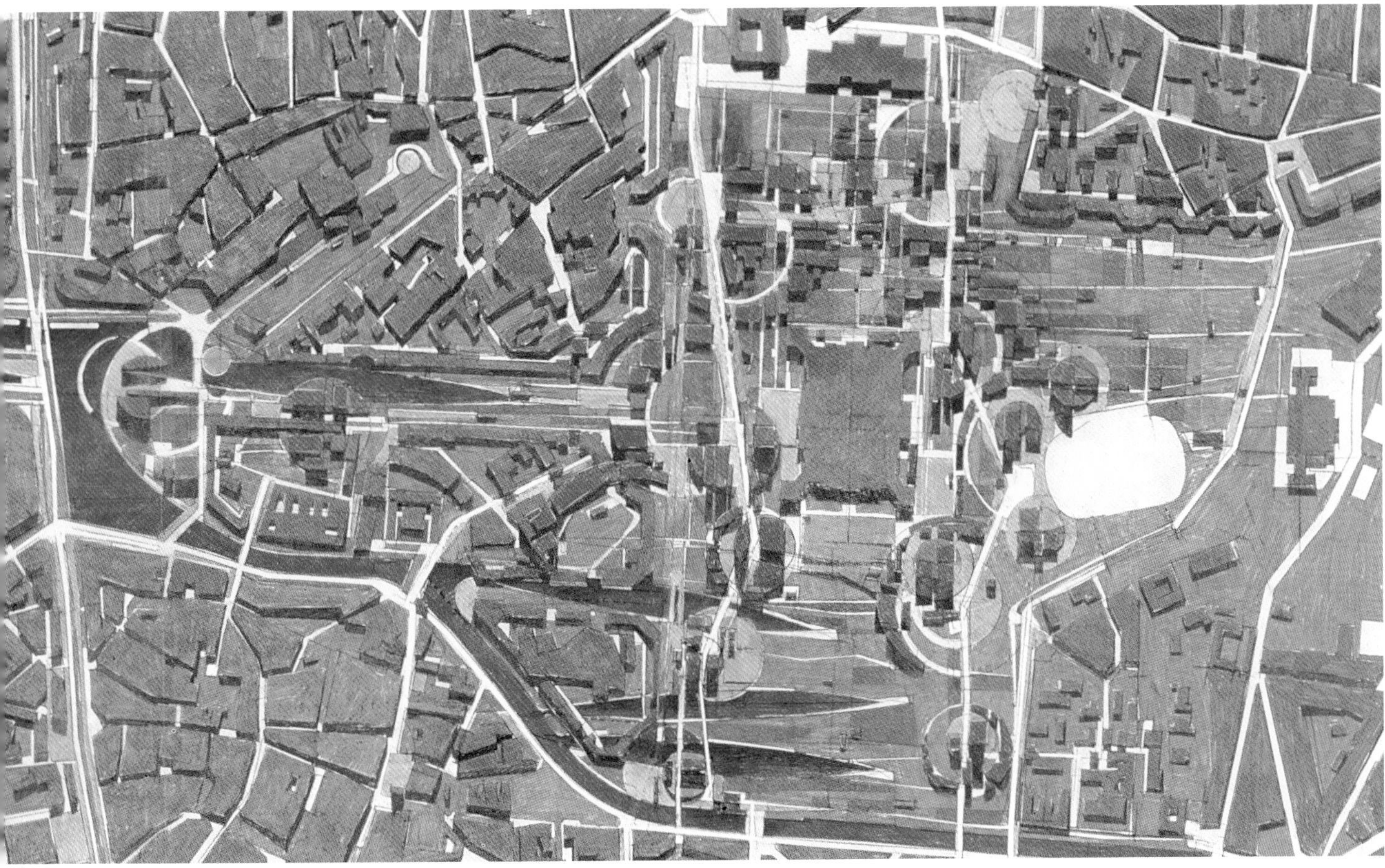

110
Bucharest 2020,
Bucharest, Romania,
plan of existing city center

111
Bucharest 2020,
new urban design
plan for city center

The Bucharest "2020" project is a somewhat gentle manifesto based on this approach – an "urbanagram" in overdrive. As 'monstrous', Ceauşescu's Bucharest was assessed in the Bucharest 2000 competition entry by Sorkin Studio as a significant opportunity to illustrate de-monumentalization through re-scaling, re-calibration and re-programming the city center. A series of figurative bombs were exploded around the central marble palace, which served as Ceaucescu's 'Kremlin', and the 'parade ground' entourage was liberated as public space. As with most Sorkin projects the river was utilized as a vital urban system – versus a sewer or freeway – but also as a specific means of destroying the explicit grandiosity of the totalitarian city. The river also carries metaphoric weight as an untamable 'other' in a city otherwise ritually and tragically denatured over centuries. The river basin was expanded, to incorporate amorphous green space and infiltrate the streets and city blocks, further destabilizing the pompous 'one-directionality' of the classical main axis.

Sorkin Studio plans realize maximum texture through de-centering infrastructure and sowing multiple conveyance and housing systems. These systems are variable in scale but use-specific. The automobile is typically demoted in Sorkin's urbanism and architectural montage overruns the vast corridors typically reserved for vehicular passage. Slow and fast transport systems are segregated with an emphasis on intermodal, low-tech systems within residential areas. The hysterical and the delirious montages supercede the placid statics of International Style urbanism invoking instead frisson and chaos reminiscent of Team X and Archigram but more intensely and comprehensively 'slathered on'.

The early whimsy of the Studio's work has been more recently surpassed by projects that radiate a profound desire for sustainability – a 'default' utopian spirit. Südraum Leipzig and Floating Islands, Hamburg are cases in point. The former is a grave example of monumental folly, in terms of the tragic strip mining and historical despoliation of land practiced in Eastern Germany, part of the transnational area known as the Black Triangle – a vast region between Bohemia, Silesia and Saxony. Sorkin, unlike other participants in the competition *charrette*, merely flooded the open pit mines and cut new channels to link the isolated villages more or less set adrift in the ravaged landscape. His fascination with the post-industrial edginess of the site led him to the conclusion that the earth-moving equipment might actually be saved as picturesque "dinosaurs" from a bygone era. The remaining villages and newly formed villages would become islands in a vast lake system hiding and perhaps suppressing the toxic earth beneath. As in *Local Code*, Sorkin's 1993 book on an imaginary city at 42 degrees north latitude, portions of this landscape would require a special population. The ghost villages would attract – as the underground habitations in *Local Code* – a new breed of adventurers as colonists.

Floating Islands is an example of instrumentalized landscape. The notion of floating water-purification modules, lashed together to form colonies and drifting around Binnenalster, a lake in the middle of Hamburg, plays with the double nature of landscape as a zone for inhabitation and a field of mediation for environmental and ecological forces. These devices would contain recreational opportunities – e.g. tennis, swimming, fishing – while filtering the water of the lake and stirring the imagination of the local populace to picture a more lyrical urban lifestyle.

Sorkin Studio favors broad strokes. 'Brush work' is displaced with slabs and gobs of 'paint', scraped, teased and gouged into novel representations of urbanity. A system of elegant moves is evident in recent projects that suggest a common origin in typological figuration. These gestures have a similarity insofar as they are universal figures that provide programmatic integrity across projects. Not content to dodge "the drunken taxicabs of Absolute Reality" – the blind forces shaping the cultural landscape – Michael Sorkin has kicked them out of the metropolis.

112

UNIVERSITY OF CHICAGO

An alternative master plan for the University of Chicago, the commission became a controversial critique of the *de facto* segregation of the University and Woodlawn, a neighboring African-American community. The relationship of the University's collegiate-gothic architectural fabric – arranged around quadrangles – to the broader context of urban Chicago was the impetus for Sorkin's interventions. The integrative strategies envisioned, however, directly conflicted with the sub rosa official consensus that the campus was essentially an island of civility in a troubled sector of Chicago. The campus is just south of the high commercial prospects of Lake Shore Drive and looks north rather than south for cultural sustenance.

Sorkin proposed restructuring the relationship of the campus and the surrounding city – divided north-south by the green midway leftover from the 1893 World Columbian Exposition. Through emphasizing the links to the central campus and doubling the number of college buildings south of the midway, Sorkin's plan effectively created new, elongated quadrangles at the very edge of Woodlawn. This area was also to become a front door to the campus with pedestrian bridges crossing the midway.

112
University of Chicago, Chicago, IL, masterplan

113
University of Chicago, plan of new library environs

113

By adding this layer of new building, the campus would become structurally closer to the neighborhood to its south and opportunities for mutual interaction would be enhanced. The plan also suggested that the University make specific forays into the Woodlawn district by providing new parks and selective architectural infill to the urban fabric.

Major attempts to de-monumentalize the University were proposed in the form of adding new pedestrian and recreational systems knitting together disparate parts of the sprawling campus on Lake Superior. The area surrounding the brutalist Regenstein Library was to be reconfigured through adding figural space in the form of new dorms, laboratories and an art center. This layer of new programming was meant to surround and humble the massive library complex while linking up to the greater campus through intermodal low-tech transport systems – pedestrian, bike, and cart ways as well as traditional autoroutes. These measures were contrary to the University effort to focus on large, individual new buildings by celebrity architects as a means of transforming the campus.

114

WEST SIDE WATERFRONT — NEW YORK CITY

The West Side proposal for Manhattan's benighted waterfront encompasses the pier and warehousing district from 14th Street to Battery Park City – taking in the West Village, SoHo and TriBeCa. This land is currently under revitalization as part of the Hudson River Park, a New York State-New York City joint initiative.

Sorkin envisions an intense inhabited region with a canal and jetty following the edge of the landmass, separating commuter traffic on the water from commercial traffic. The tidal waters and air space of the lower Hudson River are currently navigated by sailboats, barges, passenger ferries, tour boats and helicopters. The channel at the water's edge would provide a secondary river system for more slow-moving craft supportive of the life and work opportunities envisioned. The local Community Boards (A–Z) have generally fought any commercial encroachments on the land devoting some of the piers to recreational and light commercial enterprises (restaurants and museums). The State-City plan more or less sets the whole of the waterfront into a park system, the typical 'default' mode of passive Olmstedian parkland.

114
West Side Waterfront (Manhattan), New York City, NY, urban design plan

115
West Side Waterfront (Manhattan), Holland Tunnel exit at Canal Street

116
West Side Waterfront (Manhattan), detail of waterfront boulevard

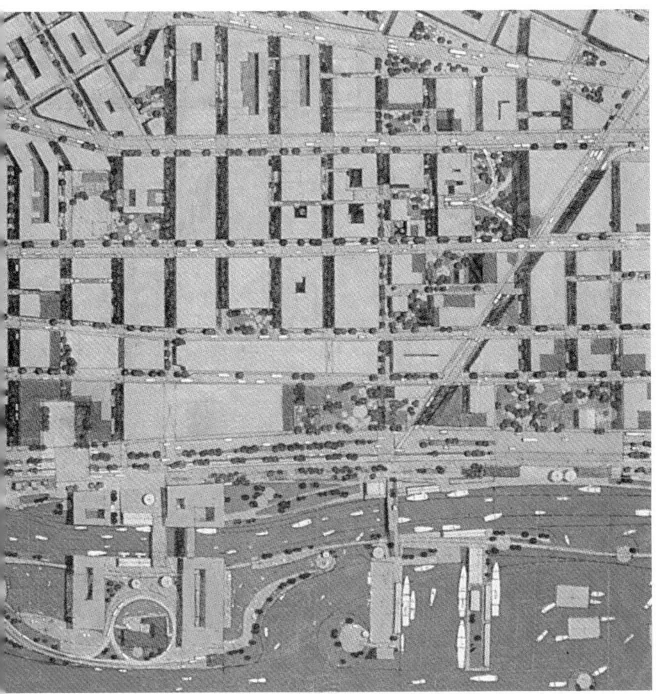

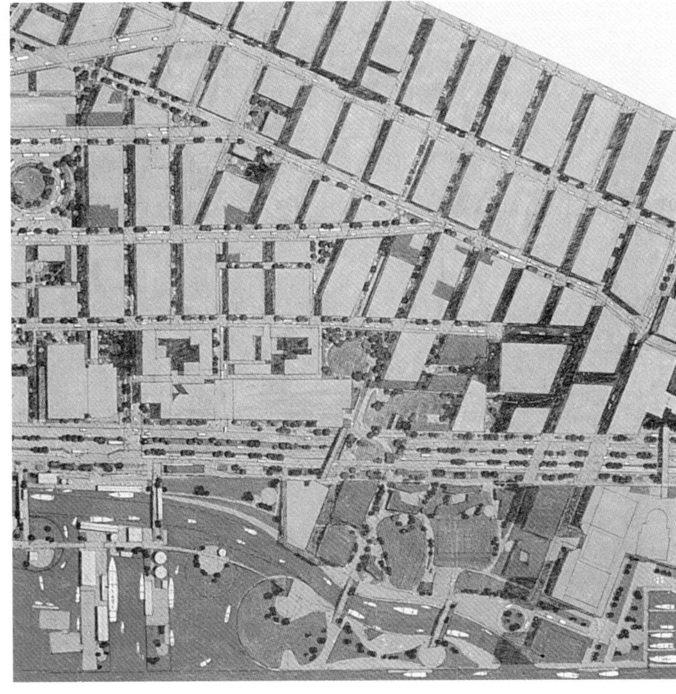

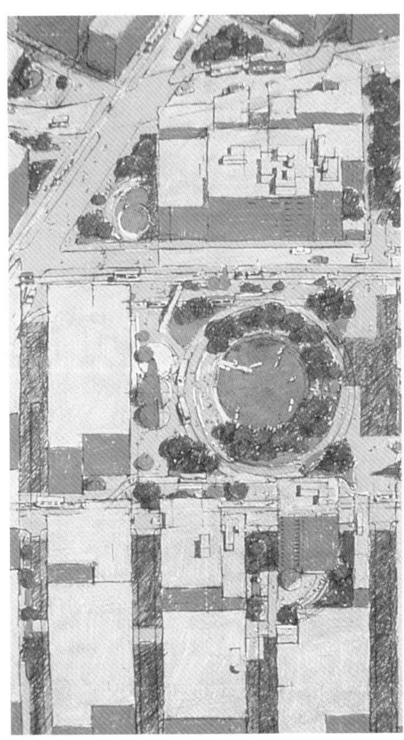

115

116

117

Sorkin also breaches the bulkhead, as much of this area is fill anyway, bringing the water into the communities as far as Sixth Avenue. The area surrounding the entrance / exit to the Holland Tunnel is singled out for a monumental water park and as a location for a new light rail terminal. This latter facility could be accommodated simply by appropriating one of the existing tubes of the Holland Tunnel. Sorkin's approach is complex versus univocal, with latent opportunities for spontaneous cultural activity within its all-encompassing form.

117
West Side Waterfront (Manhattan), 3-part panoramic collage looking east, south, west

EAST JERUSALEM

The master plan for East Jerusalem is a grand gesture of physical and political reconciliation. The strategic scale of the study implies a deconstruction or intentional appropriation of military planning modalities. Israeli military planners, using blue (Israeli) and pink (Arab) color codes, typically mapped land as a preliminary means of allocating resources and formalizing defense and security protocols.

The chief physical feature of the Sorkin proposal is the provision of a site for the Palestinian Parliament, east of the Old City but connected to the Central Business District by a new boulevard. The intervening serpentine lowland – Wadi Joz and Kidron River Valley – acts as a natural source of 'distance' within the *parti*. There is, however, no attempt to distinguish between Palestinian and Israeli settlements and the thickening of settlements along ridges and in plateaus (light pink) – east and west of the Old City – is not based on existing settlement patterns.

The plan attempts to 'secure' the edges of Jerusalem through designation of distinct desert ecology (yellow) and mediterranean ecology (light green). Within this environmental matrix – of open space and "thickened" settlements – government agencies and facilities are to be intentionally dispersed, versus concentrated, much like the original, aborted L'Enfant plan for Washington, D.C. The plan also includes hypothetical north-south and east-west rail links, tying together the now disparate units of Palestinian and Israeli settlements. A north-south rail system would ultimately link Jerusalem and Damascus (Syria), an east-west system Tel Aviv and Amman (Jordan).

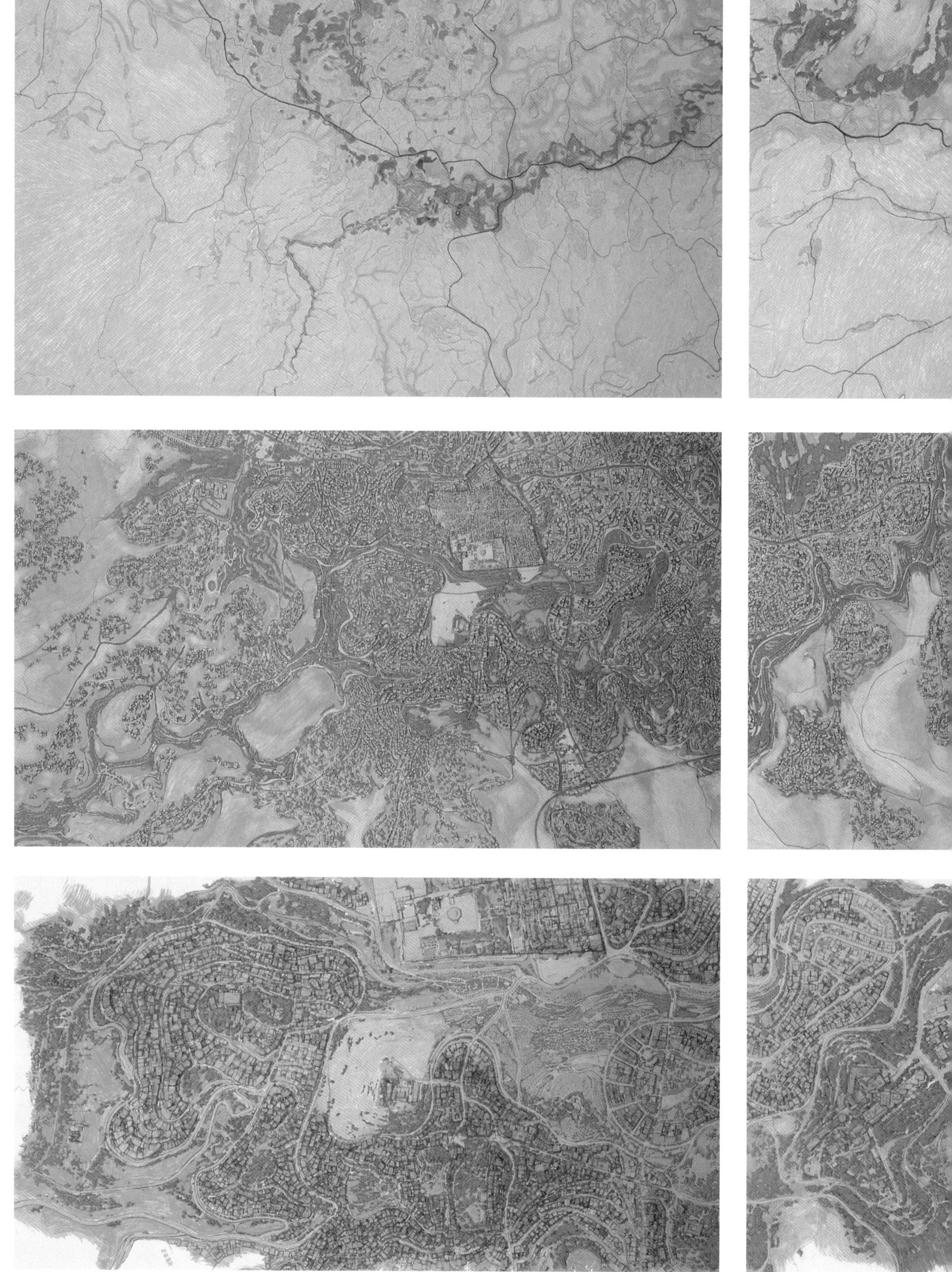

118 | 119 | 120

MICHAEL SORKIN STUDIO | 145 HUDSON STREET | NEW YORK, NY 10013
T 212 431 9120 | F 212 343 0561

MICHAEL SORKIN STUDIO is a design practice based in New York City with both practical and theoretical projects at all scales but with a special interest in urban design.
MICHAEL SORKIN received architectural training at Harvard University and MIT. He has taught, lectured and agitated all over the world. He is currently Professor of Urbanism and Director of the Institute of Urbanism at the Academy of Fine Arts in Vienna.
He has also recently been appointed Director of the Graduate Program in Urban Design at City College, New York City, New York. His influential books on urban design, rarely out of print, are exemplified by Local Code (1993), Variations on a Theme Park (1992) and Exquisite Corpse: Writing on Buildings (1991).
Sorkin Studio – Michael Sorkin, Andrei Vovk, Yukiko Yokoo, Mitchell Joachim – stretch the boundaries of contemporary urbanism through appropriation of territory. The plans and visions of the studio typically overstep and overreach the bounds of a commission and colonize the far reaches of the metropolis. Both commissioned and noncommissioned projects work hand-in-hand to foment the radical restructuring of modern urban landscape and architecture, with the intentional conflation of usually discrete instrumentalities – infrastructure, local and global ecology, office space and housing, parks and waterways.
An intense hybridization of space and building form is evident in Sorkin Studio projects – a de facto de-politicization of planning – in favor of inclusiveness and heterogeneity.

SELECTED PROJECTS

University of Chicago, Alternative Master Plan
Chicago, IL, design 1999

East Jerusalem
Israel (occupied Palestine), design 1999

Columbus Circle
New York City, NY, competition 1998

Floating Islands
Hamburg, Germany, design 1997

Friedrichshof Commune
Burgenland, Austria, design 1997

West Side Waterfront
Manhattan, New York City, NY, design c. 1997

Bucharest 2020
Bucharest, Romania, design charrette 1996

Brooklyn Waterfront
Brooklyn, NY, design c. 1994

Governors Island (Municipal Art Society Ideas Competition)
New York City, NY, competition 1996

East New York
Brooklyn, New York City, NY, design c. 1996

Neurasia
somewhere between Hong Kong and Hanoi, design 1996

Südraum Leipzig
Leipzig, Germany, design charrette, c. 1994

Souks of Beirut
Beirut, Lebanon, competition 1994

Berlin Spreebogen
Berlin, Germany, competition 1991

SELECTED BIBLIOGRAPHY

LEWIS BALTZ AND JEAN-PAUL ROBERT, "Le Triangle Noir (The Black Triangle)"
L'Architecture d'Aujourd'hui (June 1998)

JOAN COPJEC AND MICHAEL SORKIN, "Shrooms: East New York"
Assemblage (August 1994)

TSUYOSHI MATSUHATA (ED.), "Ideas and Approaches to Architecture and the City: A New U.S. East Coast Movement"
Space Design 9 (September 1994)

JAYNE MERKEL, "Modernism Redux: New York in the 1990s"
Modernism and Modernization in Architecture (London: Academy Editions, 1999)

MICHAEL SORKIN, "Westside Waterfront, Brooklyn Waterfront Governor's Island"
Abitare 384 (May 1999)

MICHAEL SORKIN, Wiggle: Michael Sorkin Studio
(New York: Monacelli Press, 1998)

MICHAEL SORKIN, Exquisite Corpse: Writing on Buildings
(New York: Verso, 1991)

MICHAEL SORKIN, Local Code
(New York: Princeton Architectural Press, 1993)

MICHAEL SORKIN (ED.), Variations on a Theme Park
(New York: Hill and Wang, 1992)

MICHAEL SORKIN, Giving Ground
(New York: Verso, 1999)

MICHAEL SORKIN, "Utopia Under Glass"
ID (September-October 1993)

GÜNTHER UHLIG, "Südraum Leipzig"
Garten + Landschaft (January 1995)

Südraum Leipzig: Eine Region im Wandel
Ergebnisse der 3. Regionalkonferenz und des Teamwettbewerbs
(Leipzig: Schäfer Verlag, 1994)

Aufriß: Künstlerische Positionen zur Industrielandschaft in der Mitte Europas
Ein Projekt der Kulturstiflumg des Freistaates Sachsen und des Siemens Kulturprogramms (Dresden: Verlag der Kunst, 1996)

"Beached Houses"
[Design citation], Progressive Architecture (January 1992)

"Michael Sorkin: Future Zones [and] Eleven Tasks for Urban Design"
Perspecta 29 (Yale University, 1998)

118
Jerusalem Masterplan, Israel & 'Palestine' plan of settlement densities

119
East Jerusalem Masterplan, plan of settlement pattern with arable land

120
East Jerusalem Masterplan (detail), plan of settlement with high-density area (with Kidron River)

PATH ONE: GEOMETRISM

ABSTRACTION AND METAPHOR

WHEN WE SPEAK THE WORD 'LIFE', IT MUST BE UNDERSTOOD WE ARE NOT REFERRING TO LIFE AS WE KNOW IT FROM ITS SURFACE OF FACT, BUT TO THAT FRAGILE, FLUCTUATING CENTER WHICH FORMS NEVER REACH. AND IF THERE IS STILL ONE HELLISH, TRULY ACCURSED THING IN OUR TIME, IT IS OUR ARTISTIC DALLYING WITH FORMS, INSTEAD OF BEING LIKE VICTIMS BURNT AT THE STAKE, SIGNALING THROUGH THE FLAMES.[1]

ANTONIN ARTAUD

The reliance on geometric forms is a type of abstraction that is systematic and often reductive to the point of eliminating difference. The underlying model of order is an approximation of an ideal that presupposes rationality as the highest good. This relative position is, however, a manifestation only of a specific type of order based on a system of assumptions.

The formalistic (the abstract) negates a whole range of options or reduces them to a schema that is both pattern and patois. This intentional proscription of context is often an after-effect of anxiety derived from a denial of influence. In extreme cases it is an absolute absence intentionally imposed on a very real presence. Its primary role is negation. As half language, the 'patois' of geometrism insinuates probity – or an aesthetic of maximum clarity – at the expense of both poetic and actual contingency and immanence. It is intrinsically anti-semantic. An effect – a metonym – for or of the quest for certitude and the absolute and pristine, geometrism often falls victim to its own inherent weakness; an unusually high rate of insipidness and, ironically, instability. In the diachronic history of gardens, for example, formal orders become a methodology for dating and locating design types. The highborn provenance of geometrism reveals a fictional site (time) outside contingency – a site synonymous with the mythic world navel. It is a syntactic field that rarely acknowledges the language it is built over – the language of things. Allied with metaphysics, geometrism is the "white light" of architectural discourse.

Proportion and symmetry are not what they appear. In fact, most schematics if turned into facts on the ground subject the varied (heterogeneous) and mutual inconsistencies of things-in-themselves to a simplistic mathematical partition, or to a calculus of returning notions of hierarchy and dependency. The less rigorous is also often the most complex by virtue of an open matrix. Such geometrism is a subtle form of mechanism – an extension into physical space of a logic that substitutes for insight into actual complex systems. Anamorphosis or the correction of perspectival forms to counter parallax and achieve a more ideal effect is often applied – chiefly as a game – to stabilize the self-conscious model of order. Conversely, shifting forms is also a means of implying contingency or difference in a highly static system. This is the origin of the shifted grid; by introducing distortional axes or forced perspectives a mode of play is located amid the characteristic sobriety of formalist logic.

There is an ironic aspect to such subterfuge – by design – in undermining the very premise of the prevailing system. Increasingly, "baroque" contrivances further the mischief without ever discarding the orchestration of abstract constructs. This mischief is a theory – an incipient knowledge – of a transmotive within the traces of design languages (the trace being the image detached from its object). The search for form (and novelty) contains its own hermetic rapture – it closes in on itself till it collapses. Artaud's enmity toward game playing, as expressed in *Le théâtre et son double* (1938), preempts this circularity by proposing a near mystical methodology – the "signaling through the flames" of the sacrificial victim, the artist. Artaud's famous comments on *Lot & His Daughters*, an apocalyptic painting in the Louvre usually attributed to Lucas van der Leyden (1494–1533), suggests that formalism in art is synonymous with the idle pleasures of the flesh. In a synchronic dimension – where time does not exist – there is an extraordinary archetypal language, which might

[1] ANTONIN ARTAUD, THE THEATRE AND ITS DOUBLE (NEW YORK: GROVE PRESS, TRANS. MARY CAROLINE RICHARDS, 1958), P. 13

be pictured as fire raining from above. The image of fire is the mystic sign of immanence, a syntagmatic gesture illuminating the inner resources of language.

Moving closer to the source than mere speculative systems, always self-conscious of the weakness of mimesis, an order that approaches the nature of things begins in a privileging not of irony but of metaphor – the favored trope of poets and mystics alike. An order of signifiers that opens the semantic field of discourse to the seeds (*semene*) or flickering flames of the Real – the things-in/of-themselves – establishes within its conceptual borders multiple centers and vectors linking worlds (and words) as works, whorls, warps, whims, waves. In essence, a surplus of wavering (in the guise of a provisionary system) is founded on a semantic field that includes the language of nature. Void and vortex substitute for figure and cosmos.

The search for a natural language – the mythic rose – is itself a metaphor for the long-anticipated advent of a unity of knowledge with the actual. This is the basis of Walter Benjamin's Coming Philosophy.[2] The abyss of subjective (negative) formulations has appeared in the place of such a language. Metaphysics is essentially a negative dialectic: a theory of types has formed, over time, as a paradigm animated by its own force of internal attraction – the magnetic resilience of types through formally diverse iterations. Giorgio Agamben, Italian editor of Benjamin's *Complete Works*, has furthered the cause and claim of this natural language, through corrective readings of Benjamin and Martin Heidegger, and made explicit the radical dimension present within language. Agamben sees in "our era an unprecedented opportunity to seize the *thus*: the pure being-in-language of the nonlinguistic".[3] Agamben's analytic – a formulation of the "coming singularity" – takes into account the transcendental history of language, which is based in a system of tropes, figures of speech and thought, that originate in the gap between the purely semiotic field of signs and the elaborate, variegated field of discourse. The specific concept of infancy that he develops is a cipher for the pure language *within* discourse, a legacy buried within signifying chains, but essentially pre-existent to discourse. The search for this pristine state was also alluded to in Wittgenstein's rigorously positivistic *Tractatus* (1921). "What Wittgenstein posits, at the end of the *Tractatus*, as the 'mystical' limit of language is not a psychic reality located outside or beyond language in some nebulous so-called 'mystical experience', it is the very transcendental origin of language, nothing other than infancy."[4] Landscape architecture is positioned at this transcendental threshold of language as the synthesis of philosophy, science and art. The fusion of forms of knowledge is implicit in landscape architecture in that it incorporates the archaic language of the world into its diverse formulations, which are essentially the terms by which we approach the world. This epistemological essence is both the promise and the curse of design languages; the latter in cases when the language becomes incapable of transparency and becomes a system of commenting only upon its own limited resources.

A natural language is not a primitive, originary formulation suspended in the void. It is neither new nor old. It is an always-existing correspondence within things linking things. The instrumentalism of formal systems mitigates the elucidation of a natural language. Discourse and artifice are the self-perpetuating antitheses to a natural language that inheres in experience and is merely further buried by typologies, corollaries, systematics and statics. Statics, as applied to the building arts, is a science of suspending dynamics. Flows, vectors and entropic forces are blocked or diverted through structural interventions. Geometric systems are analogic static systems, picturing in schematic form the regulation or preemption of natural, 'charmed' systems. Goethe's famous observation that Strasbourg Cathedral resembled "frozen music" fully exemplifies this architectural state of suspension of forces, now in the throes of a thaw.

Giorgio Agamben pictures the origin of language in a landscape of "infancy" – a zone associated with pure historicity. "The origin of language must necessarily be located at a break with the continual opposition of diachronic and synchronic, historical and structural, in which it is possible to grasp as some kind of *Ur-event*, or *Urfaktum*, the unity-difference of invention and gift, human and non-human, speech and infancy."[5] Language has a "double signification" – the semiotic and the semantic – and "taken in itself, the sign is pure correspondence with itself, and pure difference in relation to any other sign… It exists when it is recognized as a signifier by all the members of the linguistic community… With the semantic, we enter into the specific mode of signification engendered by *discourse*."[6] This

[2] WALTER BENJAMIN, "ON THE PROGRAM OF THE COMING PHILOSOPHY" (1917–18), WALTER BENJAMIN: SELECTED WRITINGS, VOL. 1, ED. MARCUS BULLOCK & MICHAEL W. JENNINGS (CAMBRIDGE: HARVARD UNIVERSITY PRESS, 1998)

[3] GIORGIO AGAMBEN, THE COMING COMMUNITY, TRANS. MICHAEL HARDT (MINNEAPOLIS: UNIVERSITY OF MINNEAPOLIS PRESS, C. 1993), UNPAGINATED

[4] GIORGIO AGAMBEN, INFANCY & HISTORY: ESSAYS ON THE DESTRUCTION OF EXPERIENCE (LONDON: VERSO, 1993), P. 51

[5] GIORGIO AGAMBEN, IBID, PP. 49–50

[6] EMILE BENVENISTE, CITED BY AGAMBEN, IBID, P. 54

site of language within the "historico-transcendental" realm of infancy is marked by phonemes, "those differential signs that are both 'pure and empty' and 'signifying and non-signifying'." Belonging to neither the semiotic nor to the semantic, phonemes "are located in the correspondence-difference (in the *chora*, as Plato would have said) between the two regions, in a 'site' which can perhaps be described only in its topology and which coincides with that historico-transcendental region – before the subject of language and without somatic substance – which we have defined above as human *infancy*."[7]

By closely describing the topography of this nether region, Agamben has exposed the building stones of discourse. The basic units – the phonemes – "enable the passage from the semiotic to the semantic". Such base units of language are present in every developed language – architectural or otherwise. Language also contains the possibility of remaining mute, a potential state within the closed world of signs. "Every language that is wholly contained within a single dimension (whether it is the chirp of the cricket or sign systems employed by man other than language) necessarily remains within the semiotic... Only human language, as something belonging to both the endosomatic and the esosomatic, adds another sense to semiotic meaning, transforming the closed world of the sign into the open world of semantic expression."[8] The profoundly poetic language of conceptual art – inclusive of architecture – derives its power by operating at the threshold of the semantic. This threshold is the site of the metaphoric flame – that essence which Artaud's critique would make us submissive to. For Walter Benjamin, restoring essence to past works of art – and to the newly formed – is the sole task of criticism: "Thus the critic inquires about the truth whose living flame goes on burning over the heavy logs of the past and the light ashes of life gone by."[9]

If a building or constructed landscape pictures active forces it reflects the consonance of the natural order and the chains of signifiers within discourse. If it embodies implicit, passive forces it employs this natural language of pure signs, which by no means implies it is a natural system. On the contrary, all architectures – even minimalist architectures – are highly synthetic and may utilize non-organic and anorganic principles, methodologies and materials. Artist and critic Peter Halley's remarks on the "entropic and catatonic" nature of minimalist art suggest that minimalist art crossed into the mute territory of abstraction as a reaction to the strenuous polemics of abstract expressionism.[10] A natural language of things is not a mimetic language, after nature, but a potent, integral language of forces, figures and concepts. Ecology has been repeatedly misrepresented as a virtuous language of things outside the cultural milieu of human semantic systems. This naïve conceptual apparatus produced patently blind systems that mimicked but did not actualize the full, open nature of the natural orders admired and imitated. Cultural landscape is no less an ecological process even if it is built on top of the environmental aspects of first nature. An ecology of cultural systems is neither trope nor scientific subject – it is instead a feature of an as yet unrecognized totality of nesting systems, part contrived, part given. (The latter – the given – are of such antiquity that the origins are perceived as timeless.) "Archaic" topology subsists in an imaginary tableau "above" or "below" the otherwise ordered, agreeable systems of everyday experience.

The so-called monstrous nature of the "archaic" realm is in fact a function of a specific subjectivity, a collective subjectivity with monstrous features of its own coinciding with the entropic disorders of the natural world. Fauve design styles play with the figurative power of the monstrous, a function of mechanistic naturalism. This is precisely the realm of play that animates subjectivity locked exclusively within a closed field – the field of play of the psychotic subject no longer integrated with the world. The social or political analog is the experience of phantasm at the aesthetic level. Phantasm introduces aspects of perverse charm to the static, homogeneous everyday experience of the world – the bourgeois flirtation with radicalism and/or the subcultural is but one example. Phantasm is the introjection of remote images of disorder, distemper, disease and dystopia into everyday consciousness. Ennui, in design disciplines, breeds an instrumental and safe architectural temporalism, which in turn motivates new heresies in the avant-garde, where, today, radicalism is most often a style versus a return to the atomic principles of semantic renovation and revolution.

Landscape architecture – a lyric formalism resembling the late Romantic and post-Romantic music of composers Anton Bruckner and Gustav Mahler – incorpo-

[7] AGAMBEN, IBID, P. 58

[8] AGAMBEN, IBID, PP. 58–59

[9] WALTER BENJAMIN, CITED IN AGAMBEN, IBID, P. 122

[10] PETER HALLEY, "BEAT, MINIMALISM, NEW WAVE AND ROBERT SMITHSON", PETER HALLEY, COLLECTED ESSAYS: 1981–1987 (NEW YORK: SONNABEND GALLERY & LAPIS PRESS, 1989), PASSIM

rates the archaic history of the world into present-dayness through symbolic and 'symphonic' topology. Landscape architecture is inherently a philosophy of language – a form of Philology – writ large.

The critique of geometrism is less a denunciation of formalism than a call to reinvest geometry with inherent ethical, figurative and cultural significance – immanence. Modernity in landscape architecture has adopted the denatured systems of logic and positivism while jettisoning the inherent symbolic and latent figurative language of geometric forms. As vestibule to philosophy – in neo-platonic exegesis – geometry was a secret language of forms significantly intertextual and, in part, a synthetic language of ethical precepts. Immanence in modernity and post-modernity is systematically repressed, versus cultivated, as an element of cultural knowledge. The epistemological content of modernity is tragically situated outside the work of art in the critical apparatus of the art world. To restore immanence, forms must speak their own language, their own terms, directly and contingently, in the very facts of their existence. This estimation of the language of forms is the ever-present potential of art and architecture – the restoration of presence to absence.

The post-structural anxiety concerning the ability of language to say anything concrete and the positivist reduction of language to a system of formal signs is negated in the hypothetical restoration of semantic presence to environmental systems. Making language concrete circumvents skepticism, associated with critiques of types of knowledge, and infers the originary prescience of elementary formal systems. The irreparable gap in representational systems may be collapsed to its utmost salience by stripping discourse of its self-referential, existentialist anomie. In place of discourse may appear, then, the *Urfaktum* – the natural largess of forms that underwrites all developed, differentiated and critical systems of rhetoric. Landscape, as a proto-metaphorical system of rhetoric, transports the subject to the vicinity of the object through a presentation of signs that short-circuit the circular hermeneutics of critical discourse. Such signs are mostly borrowed and contain aeons of implicit historicity. They are the 'flashing' signals of a language of experience of the world buried in the meta-logical abstractions that commonly substitute for experience.

TOWARDS A GRAMMAR OF NATURAL LANDSCAPE

EACH PORTION OF MATTER MAY BE CONCEIVED AS A GARDEN FULL OF PLANTS, AND AS A POND FULL OF FISH. BUT EVERY BRANCH OF EACH PLANT, EVERY MEMBER OF EACH ANIMAL, AND EVERY DROP OF THEIR LIQUID PARTS IS IN ITSELF LIKEWISE A SIMILAR GARDEN OR POND.[11]

G. W. LEIBNIZ

The Baroque mathematician and philosopher Gottfried Wilhelm Leibniz (1646–1716) functions today in architectural discourse as the progenitor of a theory of a complex, universal syntax rooted in mathematical topography. Of prime cultural significance is Leibniz's position at the separation of natural and moral philosophy in the Baroque era. Architectural production today has adopted his deterministic, vitalistic "calculus" (by way of Gilles Deleuze and Henri Bergson) as a means of reconstituting a dynamic praxis within a highly rationalized profession. Architecture – an implicitly ethical activity – is prone to cyclic disturbances to the normative, classicizing aspects of the larger corpus. Classicism, as a high form of any style (Giorgio Vasari), invokes disturbances from below and within. Baroque architect Francesco Borromini, as well as Mannerist architects of the 16th century, likewise disrupted the placid statics of Renaissance perspectivism for both implied and substantive ethical reasons via enmity and anxiety.

Leibniz has gained currency today for the exceptional fluidity and implicit anti-tectonic nature of his thought. Unlike Kant's clearly delineated world of limitations (categories), Leibniz's universe is a non-architectonic continuum or union of forms rooted in a theory of "pos-

[11] G. W. LEIBNIZ, MONADOLOGIE (1714), CITED IN GILLES DELEUZE, THE FOLD: LEIBNIZ AND THE BAROQUE (MINNEAPOLIS: UNIVERSITY OF MINNESOTA PRESS, 1993), P. 9

sible worlds" or alternative universes – paths not taken – which as variations on the Real would produce a fatal rupture in the harmony of the world we inhabit. Leibniz's differential calculus – with its curves and splines – mirrors this worldview that *approaches* but does not *apprehend* a grammar of the cultural world. However, mathematics lacks a semantic field and is merely a language given by nature – it is, in essence, "closed" or "mute". The seductive appeal of "pleated" mathematical and natural forms belies the overarching mediation of number and the alleged latent instrumentalism within Leibniz's essentialist – Rosicrucian – model. A system of monadic forms – in constant motion and mutually mirroring one another ad infinitum – Leibniz's universal syntax neither anticipates the inspired instrumentalism of quantum mechanics nor the necessary value (as yet undecipherable) due non-uniform and fluctuating fields (those figures that haunt particle physics, chaos theory and fractal geometry). Leibniz's model is the baroque machine but detailed in minute particulars and so closely integrated that the structure appears uniform and contiguous. The mere plaything of architects, the appropriation of this model and of chaos theory and quantum mechanics serve more as dynamite, to destroy normative statics, than as grounds for innovative theoretical constructs to be applied to building more vital environments.

Perhaps semiotics and the otherwise linguistic tools of structuralism and post-structuralism came closest to revealing the grammar of natural language in this century. The resistance to this school of thought in architecture was primary formed through opposition to the application of linguistic devices to design. Such opposition, however, read semiotics from within the narrow confines of pragmatics. The application of critical tools to the received forms of architectural design is and was rarely an attempt to construct form but instead to read, interpret and influence form. As pragmatic tools, semiotics and deconstruction eventually simply fall away – a type of temporary scaffolding. The results on tectonics are well known, as are the effects of intentional and unintentional misprision on built systems. Unfortunately, the liberties taken with architectural syntax more than justify skepticism. Deep structures remain elusive, if not mythical, and the grammar of architecture, on the other hand, is also intrinsically instrumental. It does not coincide with the Real nor does the theorization of the same justify design by narrative or other well-meant semantic circumlocutions. For we are merely imposing further subjective complexes onto an indefinable field. Cartesian and post-Cartesian subjects, we are haunted by what Slavoj Žižek has identified as the persistence of the "indivisible remainder" – abject subjectivity.[12] His writings, insistently Lacanian, constantly circle the rupture in the Real that has produced the complexes of the Big Other, a system of superstructures that mediate everyday experience. Transcending the transfixed state of modern subjectivity, the field of discourse becomes quite literally 'wide open' for improvisation and, as Nietzsche prophesized, very clever antics upon the pre-existent scaffolding – rehearsals upon the stage set established aeons ago in our first confrontations with the nature of things.

The first order of change in contemporary landscape involves the deconstruction of geometrism – axial and proportional systems are opened to alternative systems typified by a new topographics that is sculptural and evocative. Euclidean space and baroque (axial) space is collapsed or invaded by undulating landforms, curving vertical and horizontal vectors, and planting systems drawn not from notational orders derived from modules and effects of serial extension but from readings of site, history, environment and overlapping contingencies. Plant communities and environmental systems – still of an imposed order – substitute for measured, abstract systems drawn from a grid or a linear disposition derived (left over) from Renaissance and Baroque schematics.

Plant systems and landforms introduce, with the addition of rhetorical or figurative artistic forms, a language of site consistent with readings of heterogeneous factors. An implicit phenomenology is evident versus or in conjunction with abstract imposed structural changes. In urban design these factors are highly synthetic, often symbolic gestures situated in a language of resistance (or hypertextual metalanguage) circumventing the often gratuitous and predictable quotidian experience of economically and socially determined environments. Sinuous forms – in themselves – are meaningless unless formulated on a theory of attraction (that they influence the re-making if not the re-reading of an environment ruled by orthodoxy – i.e. economic, social and aesthetic claims).

Planting systems that are predicated on ecological principles in urban settings are at best picturesque if sited

[12] SLAVOJ ŽIŽEK, THE INDIVISIBLE REMAINDER (LONDON: VERSO, 1996), PASSIM. SEE ALSO THE TICKLISH SUBJECT: THE ABSENT CENTRE OF POLITICAL ONTOLOGY (LONDON: VERSO, 1999), PASSIM

as evidence of a local, pre-existing type. When tied to more evocative and critical design elements the plant syntax develops semantic and intertextual import. This importation of metaphorical content is an incendiary activity when linked to a close reading of public space in the increasingly commercialized urban landscape. Readings of post-industrial or otherwise ravaged sites in urban and ex-urban settings begin at the most salient topographic level – the stark landscape of casual dishevelment – moving up the ecological chain to horticultural, hydrological and cultural artifacts (fragments) while retaining the surreal aspects of an environment essentially exposed, denatured and disenchanted. Land Art borrowed the cultural anxiety associated with despoiled land for substantial firepower, fueling a polemic aimed at modern utopias. Smithson famously positioned himself between the ecologist and the industrialist. It is here, in this intertextual, semantic field of figurative discourse, that an ethical language is implanted.

This all then seems a circling and observation of multiple histories and virtual contingencies. The readings of site that qualify design initiatives remain in a space of interpretation, a bracketing of objective forces, as a strategic alliance with the indeterminate nature of cultural systems. Nature as a systematic paradigm is not in fact the point of departure it was in the past several decades nor is pure art the motivation of new landscape. In between architecture and landscape a wealth of overlapping concerns mirrors the speculative (perhaps mannerist) ethos of the post-cultural condition. Aesthetic pursuits that embrace both existing conditions and structuralist methodologies in pursuit of synthesis, or a new (hybrid) culture, are processes of becoming that mirror the secret nature of things.

ACCEPTING THE INCOMMENSURABLE

CLARITY ENDLESSLY PLUNGES INTO OBSCURITY.[13]

GILLES DELEUZE

Cultural systems in landscape are often borrowed or stolen from related and unrelated fields. Discourse has presented a plethora of options, tangents to a purely aesthetic or functional approach. Transmotives animate an analogical melding of purpose and program in urban design systems that reach beyond the prosaic production of space to, instead, systems of critique and resistance (and synthesis).

The normative practice of urban design, after the momentous mid-twentieth century decades of urban renewal, presented itself as a byproduct of commercial and corporate expansionism. The enduring legacy of massive infrastructural projects was followed by a ubiquity of uniformity (the corporate plaza and the glassed atria of urban commercial zones). All-pervading and all-embracing, microtexture and local difference survived only beyond the red line of financial zones in the interstices of developing economic regimes. The rediscovery of Situationist motives in recent years has bred a new appreciation of resistance to the denatured urban landscape of corporatism. Situationism, as second-generation Surrealism, viewed the city as unbridled spectacle, creating in response anti-spectacle.

Cultural systems emerge, on the other hand, from historical and subcultural currents – once marginal and later absorbed into the paradigmatic aesthetic regime by reverse colonization and authorization of exceptional stature within the over-aesthetic. The usurpation of the under-aesthetic (e.g. *film noir* or the dark novels and short stories of Dashiell Hammett where a "vision of a precarious, random world" rules[14]) by the paradigmatic regime is the equivalent of the return to wild nature for new breeding stock. Urban colonization follows certain patterns if not laws, flows from overheated to cool zones, marked by economic and cultural opportunism. Landscape appropriates subcultures in both ways, as a means of invoking vitality and as a means of normalizing unruly conditions outside the paradigmatic.

The least appealing approach to absorbing difference is through apprehension and colonization. The syntagmatic (horizontal) relations of instrumentalism (not a

[13] GILLES DELEUZE, THE FOLD: LEIBNIZ AND THE BAROQUE, P. 32

[14] MICHIKO KAKUTANI, "SOCIETY'S DARK CORNERS SEEN THROUGH KEYHOLES", THE NEW YORK TIMES (FRIDAY, AUGUST 27, 1999), P. E43

claim or act of colonization) include the introduction of linkages between and through formerly distinct (fragmented) cultural systems. In adding a vital chain of ecological signifiers (fauna, plants, landform, water) the topographic language bridges difference without actual formal colonization and exploitation (the commercial-civic idiom), e.g. the recent re-introduction of falcons to New York's Central Park or the cultivation of 'meadows' in London's Kew Gardens.

This sometimes vital, sometimes trivial bridging initiative excludes the imposition of *literal* narrative (forms of ideology), which merely imposes an imaginary or authorized biographic element on the ground. Historic sites are all too often coded in this narrative way with figures of speech that, in being borrowed or stolen, overemphasize or overwhelm an intrinsically historic aura. Reliant on complex interpretive apparatus, the narrative landscape is an artful dodging of the essentially heterogeneous nature of all sites. Whose history? or Whose narrative? is a valid question when program collides with constituency. There is only so much writing in the landscape that may instill confidence before it devolves to mimic *plein-air* advertising or corporate theme parks with the pictured lavish sensibility of consumerism. Consuming history is as appalling a construct as may be imagined for the production of landscape.

Horizontal (syntagmatic) systems integrated with vertical (paradigmatic) systems – a plurality and overabundance of signifiers – is in fact a valid methodology for implying complexity and mutability. The nature of things is an amalgam of forces and constructs that are intertwined and evolving, and in essence self-regulating (the so-called 'charmed' nature of organic systems). Human intervention is but one element of a calculus of natural fields foreshadowed in Leibniz's circular mathesis. A pretended writing zero degree is but a noble game in writing landscape – the 'paper' is instrumentalized as a supposedly featureless tableau, which in fact it is not. An infinitesimal array of circular signifiers approaches critical mass in systems that flirt with but in time acknowledge and accept incommensurability.

If landscape is to approach the incommensurable, the featureless tableau (Malevich's white) or the *tabula rasa* needs qualification. The qualifications are the closest attainable point to this magnificent distance in things. The aesthetic gaze is the closest *existential* approach possible to primordial 'fire'. The near and the far, the paradigmatic and the syntagmatic merge in the iconic, imaginary space of conception where bridge transects vortex and topographics imbricate void.

CRITICAL IDEALISM

After Kant, idealism was conditioned by the categorical imperatives of skepticism and modernity's obsession with forms of knowledge remained haunted by the subjective distance between concept and world. Post-Kantian critical idealism – represented by the works of Ernst Cassirer, Aby Warburg, Erwin Panofsky, Suzanne Langer, and others – produced a critique of symbolic and cultural orders that coincided with systems of instrumental discourse. Structural linguistics, structural anthropology, hermeneutics, and phenomenology mapped the topological nature of cultural systems but – tautologically – remained a closed system or a synthetic, often capricious analytical system consistent with subjectivity. It is the concept of time, however, enshrined in rationalist systems, which produces this formalist landscape. The formal construction of time underwrites the entire range of geometrical and analytical projections that come to rest in abstract diagrams of the world.

Altering conditions of subjectivity itself involves altering the mode for perceiving the world. Shifting the locus of identity from the fixed image of self – as an object in diachronic time – to the indecidable threshold of language at the place of taking-place, the experience of time itself is altered. The subjective map of the world – landscape in its ontological sense – need not remain in a closed state of denatured, solipsistic signifiers but may chart and trace the shape of things in eternal flux. De-racinating forms of knowledge liberates the profound intertextual field of signifying subjects and the animated network of subconscious forms and forces that subsidize both the natural and man-made worlds. This mythic zone in language is the nursery of artistic and philosophical desire and its recovery is the justification for all exercises in deconstructing mechanisms of domination and regulation – from medieval heresy to modern-day post-structuralism – from Giordano Bruno to Walter Benjamin to Michel Foucault and Pierre Bourdieu. This is also why the 'Garden of Paradise' remains the oldest and most radical map of the world. Dante's *Paradiso* closed the medieval historical cycle; von Kleist's invocation of a back door to Eden in his

[15] STANLEY CAVELL, THE SENSES OF WALDEN: AN EXPANDED EDITION (CHICAGO: UNIVERSITY OF CHICAGO PRESS, 1992), PASSIM

Marionettentheater anticipated the end of modernity. Both exploit this mythic position at the world navel as a corrective. Anterior and posterior to modernity, both figurative instantiations suggest that Paradise is an always already existing territory within the synchronic, timeless dimension of human discourse.

Thoreau's plumbing the depths of Walden Pond, in *Walden* (1854), to determine the real versus the legendary depth, was a conscious symbol for approaching the reality that is always at least one stage removed from our experience of the world. In *The Senses of Walden* Stanley Cavell exposed the primal purposes of Thoreau's writing.[15] The writer of Walden sensed, and regretted, a tragicomic missed opportunity in 19th-century America to reach the metaphoric ground of things, as the nation hurtled toward the destruction of so-called wilderness. "The natural world, beyond language and theory, in its details, its very materiality of rocks and trees, was something to which the isolated self could connect in a kind of passionately ecstatic embrace."[16] For Thoreau, the natural world was the essential experience of the world – a view later absorbed by Frederick Law Olmsted, albeit a view in Olmsted's case based on creative artifice and sublimations of historicity. For Emerson nature was a book to be studied and read – a text that supported all other texts. This ideal was more staunchly romantic than Thoreau's anarchic, proto-phenomenological worldview. Thoreau's view disemboweled discourse in search of traces of first nature. It was revolutionary versus enlightened and genteel. This view lies buried – below positivism and individualism – in the American experience.

[16] DAVID LEYENSON, "DISCORD IN CONCORD", THE BOSTON BOOK REVIEW, (OCTOBER 1999), P.27

[17] JEAN-PHILIPPE ANTOINE, "'I WANT TO MAKE A PHOTOGRAPH': PHOTOGRAPHY, LANDSCAPE AND NATURE IN THE WORK OF GERHARD RICHTER", PAGES PAYSAGES 5 (1994–95), P.50

VEILED SYSTEMS

TO PAINT A LANDSCAPE VEILED IN MIST IS TO DECLARE THE VEIL, WHICH AFFECTS THE VERY ACT OF VIEWING, AND TO REFUSE TO ALLOW ITS SELF-CANCELLATION IN THE DETERMINATION OF THE OBJECT.[17]

JEAN-PHILIPPE ANTOINE

The paintings of Gerhard Richter visually propose endless qualifications through the appropriation and recalibration of photographic pictorialism. The landscapes in particular destroy the premise of the image being derived from any object and instead represent the second or third remove of the artistic gaze. The idealization of the image is destroyed through intervening and disrupting conditions. The resultant image is then a pure sign of only itself and the "image disincarnates the real".[18] Here the qualifications exert primacy within the field of landscape painting with exceptional eloquence. Richter's blurred landscapes – derived from his interpretations of the work of Caspar David Friedrich – significantly embrace contingency and undermine the privileging of the eye producing a veiled, muted view of ostensibly predictable content. The art of painting so cherished by abstract expressionists and their universalizing tendencies becomes, with Richter, an exceptional state *within* painting: their approach qualifies the object of the visual field without using acute self-referential tactics that would assume primacy within the production of the image. Richter on the contrary steps back to the edge of painting, to the mimetic frontier, and reiterates in pigment the conditions of seeing through the medium of painting, the condition of painting as a reflection several times removed from the act of seeing. The painting stands in the way of seeing. "Painting seems to be making every effort to achieve an objectivity which remains structurally beyond its reach."[19] While Friedrich deified the veil (Nature), Richter utilizes the conditions of the veil to render "the relationship between reality and the image of reality indecidable".[20]

This obstruction of seeing clearly is a condition of distance – both a metaphysical and contingent distance. It represents a critique of the condition of the purely visual – aesthetic – reductionism present within painting, and, by extension, within the act of seeing. It suggests a point within being that is irreducible – the site of that Cartesian subject that haunts all post-cultural attempts to break the solipsistic chains of aesthetic production, including philosophy. "The act of painting establishes a certain relation to the preexistence of vision, and to the division it produces."[21] This division is the subjective center, the *oculus* of all perception (of

[18] EMMANUEL LEVINAS, "REALITY AND ITS SHADOW", LEVINAS READER, ED. SEAN HAND, TRANS. ALPHONSO LINGIS (OXFORD: BASIL BLACKWELL, 1989), CITED IN THOMAS CARL WALL, RADICAL PASSIVITY: LEVINAS, BLANCHOT, AND AGAMBEN (ALBANY: SUNY, 1999), P. 17

[19] JEAN-PHILIPPE ANTOINE, OP. CIT., P.47

[20] IBID, P.52

perspective), the center of the spiritual circle that has its center everywhere and its circumference nowhere (Marsilio Ficino). In essence, the subjective center is an elemental abstraction that haunts being. A type of apostrophe, it preempts the emergence of the Real. As a form of elision, it joins unrelated but sequential figures of thought. Abstraction is the foundation of metaphysics (the fictive center that regulates all phenomena through its assumption of omniscience).

Landscape architecture is more a process of restoration – reclamation – than absolute making. It reassembles parts once of common assemblage or it combines parts in wholly new, synthetic formulations. It reveals hidden symmetries, proportional systems, or elucidates possible scenarios. By the art of assemblage, it convenes significance within the ordinary. It adds human artifice to natural largess, or subtracts complications and redundancies to clarify unity and relationship. It plays with light and shadow, organizes disparate units in chains of significance, enhances and channels atmospheric and terrestrial effects. Within the boundaries of a provisional art form the always implicit language of things is rewritten – as diatribe, joke, lecture, poem, essay and tract. Reconstituting the world, landscape architecture joins together unfathomable flows, indecipherable systems and purely imaginary precepts. It borrows the immense wealth of forms preexistent to its own emergence from the abstract wilderness within language.

In the wake of modern skepticism, after Immanuel Kant's *Critique of Pure Reason* (1781) that posits an unbridgeable distance between human subjectivity and things-in-themselves (*noumena*), language is not impotent but has now to do "with the 'terms' we strike with existence."[22] As such, perception (*phenomena*) haunts being and epi-phenomena condition human experience. Landscape architecture, as epi-phenomenon, bears witness to the elementary role of human cognition – the subjective survey of experience – without laying claim to a transcendent role in constructing the world. In describing the terms of existence, landscape architecture is however capable of re-inscribing the singular nature of being in significant chains of representation. This cultural significance is arguably unparalleled in provisionary human systems. It is consistent with Emersonian self-reliance in the sense that landscape architecture produces "objects of contemplation" which acquaint us with ourselves and extend our being.[23] Emerson's obsession with the enigmatic face of Nature – his celebration of the mysterious language of natural forms – was post-Kantian subjectivity itself reified. This inescapable condition is the foundation of all landscape architectural representations, U-topias notwithstanding. It is necessary then to answer Allen S. Weiss's speculations regarding a hypothetical garden of Pascal, as the antithesis of the Cartesian garden (*Mirrors of Infinity*, 1995).

[21] BIRGIT PELZER, "THERE IS NO THERE: GERHARD RICHTER AT THE CARRE D'ART IN NIMES", IN GERHARD RICHTER: 100 PAINTINGS, EDITED BY HANS-ULRICH OBRIST (OSTFILDERN-RUIT: CANTZ, 1996), P.136

[22] CARY WOLFE, "ALONE WITH AMERICA: CAVELL, EMERSON, AND THE POLITICS OF INDIVIDUALISM", NEW LITERARY HISTORY, 25 (1994), P.139

[23] IBID., P.143

THE OPEN SECRET

OUR INTELLIGENCE STANDS IN THE ORDER OF INTELLIGIBLES JUST WHERE OUR BODY DOES IN THE VAST REALM OF NATURE.[24]

BLAISE PASCAL

Such a garden would not be an image of Arcadia nor of Eden. It would contain the essential mark of the *aporia*, sign of a non-self-reliant subject and of doubt in the assumptions of systems. It might take the form of an ellipse – having two centers – tugged at from opposing, unknown forces. It might contain a central fountain (from Provence, bought in Paris during World War II). It might be surrounded by an aerial hedge, a double planting of European Hornbeam (*Carpinus betulus*), clipped with distinctive originality to partly close, partly open the garden to the outside world and picturing anxiety in the face of the infinite. It might contain grotesque masks spouting water, caricatures of the human condition. These masks may in turn be removed, being judged too garish and monstrous. It might be the most architectonic element of an otherwise romantic enclave surrounded by woods, neighboring a cemetery noted for its sublime pastoral atmosphere, the burial place of founding fathers. And it might be associated with a house on a hill with a notable library and gallery. It would certainly be the type of garden to haunt at night, illicitly, climbing the perimeter wall and arriving

[24] BLAISE PASCAL, PASCAL'S PENSÉES (1669), TRANS. H. F. STEWART (NEW YORK: PANTHEON, 1950), P. 25

uninvited. It would fascinate, but fail to give up its secret to imitators. It would be much admired, measured and even copied but never fully realized elsewhere. Its identity and location would be an open secret, though public it would be known to a few. It would suggest a numerical system but at once conceal that system. It would resemble the *giardino segreto* of the Renaissance but in fact present a dual, open nature. It might appear as a secret archive, built up over several incarnations, but in fact be of quite recent provenance. In a word, it would speak the secret language of the world.

PATH TWO: LEAPING AHEAD

OUTSIDE THE PARADIGMATIC

THAT TIME WHICH WE REALLY IMPROVE, OR WHICH IS IMPROVABLE, IS NEITHER PAST, PRESENT, NOR FUTURE.[25]

HENRY DAVID THOREAU

Going beyond the self-imposed limitations of the ontological analytic of Martin Heidegger's *Being and Time*, into the semantic field (the wordliness of things), the philosophical contours of *design* become the prime animating characteristic of experience in the everyday world. Heidegger's everydayness, based on being-together-with the world, was configured as preliminary spatiality – the 'here', 'there' and 'over there'. The everydayness of experience is characterized by "publicness", which *Being and Time* describes as an "averageness" or a "leveling down". The "they" – everyone including oneself ("Everyone is the other, and no one is himself") – constitutes an ontological publicness. "The 'they' maintains itself factically in the averageness of what is proper, what is allowed, and what is not. Of what is granted success and what is not. This averageness, which prescribes what can and may be ventured, watches over every exception that thrusts itself to the fore. Every priority is noiselessly squashed. Overnight, everything primordial is flattened down as something long since known. Everything gained by a struggle becomes something to be manipulated. Every mystery loses its power."[26]

This critique of averageness and leveling-down in turn, opens up the place of philosophy – a critique outside *Being and Time's* rigidly ontological premise. Heidegger alludes to this possible role of philosophy again and again, especially in his matter-of-fact descriptions of being's entanglement in the world – the so-called "thrownness" of being-in-the-world. In delineating the concept of being-with-one-another Heidegger identifies modes of indifference and modes of domination. A third mode is contrasted with these: "There is the possibility of a concern which does not so much leap in for the other as *leap ahead of* him, not in order to take 'care' away from him, but first to give it back to him as such." This leaping ahead "helps the other to become transparent to himself *in* his care and *free for* it."[27] This ontological leaping, transferred to the critique of everydayness, suggests the contours of an ethical premise. In later comments on language and discourse, Heidegger identifies discourse as "the 'significant' articulation of the intelligibility of being-in-the-world".[28] He also asks the critical philosophical question: "Is it a matter of chance that initially and for the most part significations are 'worldly', prefigured beforehand by the significance of the world, that they are indeed often predeterminantly 'spatial'?"[29]

Chains of signification are inherited. Aesthetic depth charges are required to alter this landscape. Philosophical 'landscape' – intelligibility itself – is the 'site' of preliminary spatial structures. Socratic philosophy, for example, deconstructed the Homeric mythic universe ushering in pre-modern rationality and, after the Enlightenment, sponsored – through its legatees – the loosing of the post-Romantic view to the archaic. The deified landscape of the Homeric universe – pictured in a Romantic mode in the paintings of Friedrich – became approachable, with the advent of Western rationality, only as an exceptional experience. Inherited systems are the essence of everydayness. Leaping ahead then equates the rewriting of spatial, 'liminal' codes – codes imbued with historicity. The Surrealist revolution of the 1920s and 1930s is but one episode in more recent attempts to encode radical contingency – the synthesis of idealism and materialism.[30] Publicness

[25] HENRY DAVID THOREAU, THE VARIORUM WALDEN (NEW YORK: TWAYNE PUBLISHERS, 1962), P. 96

[26] MARTIN HEIDEGGER, BEING AND TIME (1927), TRANS. JOAN STAMBAUGH (ALBANY: SUNY, 1996), P. 119 (I.IV)

[27] IBID, P. 115 (I.IV)

[28] IBID, P. 151 (I.V)

[29] IBID, P. 155 (I.V)

[30] A. S. HAMRAH, "A PARADE FLOAT, A TIME BOMB", THE BOSTON BOOK REVIEW (OCTOBER 1999), P. 6

in itself is a zone of being and as averageness is incapable of the exceptional. The exceptional can only be absorbed into this everydayness – it is unstable. A paradigmatic sameness guarantees an everydayness that is *temporally* stable. The loosing of heterogeneity and multiplicity pushes everyday experience outside the paradigmatic. The paradigmatic shifts, by degrees, and the everydayness returns anew.

EVERYDAY LANDSCAPES

Landscape then would appear to have invisible and visible structure, philosophical and physical contours. Landscape is unique in that it absorbs and pictures things-in-themselves, a form of assemblage that *inserts* whole and fragmentary natural histories within a history of form that is elemental in its basic, spatially determined topology. Present-day publicness, or picturesque averageness, is countered by concepts of wilderness, or virtual sublimity. It is also countered by the uncanny and historically sublime post-industrial wasteland of brownfields and decaying infrastructure – a different form of wilderness. Publicness currently poses a threat to both forms of sublime and exceptional landscape experience (wilderness) through appropriation and assimilation. Eco-tourism, development and global pollution threaten the former while re-development threatens the latter.

The post-industrial zones of urban and ex-urban America are prime sites for new recreational and commercial facilities. Such nether zones, economically marginalized in the new global economy, will be 'leveled' and inducted into averageness should the purely picturesque paradigm prevail. These sublime landscapes will fall into a more vital position – between ruin and reclamation – if the exceptional and uncanny aspects of their physicality are *not* absorbed into everydayness. They will instead become haunted and uninhabitable sites serving *within averageness* a purely symbolic extra-average role.

Remaining 'outside' averageness while within averageness is also a valid alternative for benighted urban housing, but at an altogether different semantic level. Absorption into the paradigmatic aesthetic is a long-term affair for such landscapes. The current trend of demolition and replacement of high-rise, public housing in American cities with low-rise, public-private townhouses and neo-traditional villages is altering the physical ground of the social and economic paradigm in essentially superficial ways. The texture of a neighborhood changes, and so does the justification for marginalization. The insertion of new housing is matched by the insertion of new large-scale commercial development, typically to pay for the urban amenities – parks, playgrounds and recreational space (including streets). The new texture is immediately – *already* – infiltrated by averageness and the paradigm of publicness dictated by the conceptualization of housing as 'markets'. Unique and exceptional character is absorbed into place names and historic sites; e.g., "Riverview" or "Ridgewood" with neither a river view nor a ridge and wood. The long-term colonization of the unique is stowed aboard the planning models in force.

'Success' is replicated in publicness. What has been deemed 'acceptable' in one location is adopted and transplanted *over and over* till it is saturated with publicness. This is the fate of waterfront plazas with tourist amenities and, quite often, prefabricated histories. The real – fishmongers, working docks and stacks of lobster traps – are absorbed by the planning model and re-engineered as restaurants, site-seeing cruises and stacks of jeans and sweatshirts. The public, sated, eventually moves on to the next incarnation of publicness, the neo-Beaux-Arts promenade by the water with rollerblading, skateboarding, jogging and dog-strolling sideshows. *Plus ça change …*

Present-day, end-of-the-millennium publicness has reached a transitional hotspot; iterations of publicness are close to exhaustion. Internet zones have supplanted real space and the density of cities has reached critical mass. New parks on post-industrial sites are returning space to publicness without encoding difference. Sameness, reification and economic anomie have exhausted themselves. This bruising critique is everywhere self-evident – it is written over and over – and the built environment is on the verge of saturation with averageness. Visual and physical signs of the virtual sale of publicness is everywhere evidenced by the abdication of public policy, in the flooding of public space with advertising and in the economic divide engulfing publicness in America.

Landscapes of resistance are formulated, against this vertical integration of publicness, on the horizontal, syntagmatic axis of difference and signification – *liter-*

ally on the horizon. These acts of turning vertical relations into horizontal relations manifest in both subtle and radical formulations. They are most evident in alternative visions for public space design – most often the *losing* entries in public design competitions. The current vogue for economic determinism in city planning – the sale of publicness – is the exhausted paradigm of verticality writ large in the landscape. The economic analytic is outside the design analytic while everywhere and in every instance shaping the outcome. The flows and folds of present-day everydayness are impregnated with layers of implicit and explicit information *spliced* onto the natural language of things. The paradox of everydayness, however, is that in every case everydayness will save itself from itself.

NEW YORK AND PRAGUE

New York and Prague – two world cities, worlds apart in their worldliness – represent on the one hand the intense capitalization of history and on the other the intense capitalization of no history and amnesia. The everydayness of Prague is embodied in its historical core, a core that is culturally closed and part of a world monument system within UNESCO. New York is the omnivorous open city, with its categorical imperative to continually reinvent itself. Its everydayness is a physical realization of the national attention-deficit disorder that obsessively forgets its own history as any and everything new sweeps away the old or absorbs it into the 'classic', a tableau of signifiers frozen in time and stripped of all exceptional status. The exceptional everydayness of Prague, with its Romanesque, Medieval, Renaissance, Baroque, Neoclassical, Constructivist, Functionalist and Social Realist center, is conversely averageness that precludes authentic experience, and – as Hélène Cixous has observed[31] – due to this historicized everydayness, the Prague that is Prague is 'nowhere' to be found. It is in the 'nowhere' or the 'mind's eye' – the proverbial eye of the beholder.

New York's extraordinary range of public spaces and its primary pedestrian culture present a tableau both paradigmatic and heterogeneous. The classic park in New York – Vaux and Olmsted's Central Park – is the paradigmatic New York outdoor space with its "green and pleasant hills" and its vast expanse countering the congestion of the Manhattan grid. In the outlying boroughs parks are likewise crisscrossed by roads and infiltrated by cultural facilities that borrow the pristine character of the Central Park model (even if they are primarily cemeteries). This paradigm conditions New York City planning of open space such that the heterogeneous, multiple incarnations of public space in the City refer endlessly to that concept of green space. The smallest parks acquire the distinctive design codes of the model down to the standard detailing and the informal apparatus of open lawn and leafy grove. This standard makes the acceptance into everydayness in New York of an alternative park model extremely difficult or exceptional. Recent planning studies have moved beyond this model but reverted to the idiomatic style after flirting with difference. The 1980s restoration of Bryant Park – after its descent into chaos – typifies the reascension of the paradigm in city planning. So too does the genteel Battery Park City esplanade, which pays tribute to 1920s New York, the time and place of the neoclassical Grand Central Terminal and the proliferation of neo-Renaissance apartment houses along Park Avenue. This re-development model was introduced, in the 1980s, in numerous American cities. It was conceived as a model of alternative publicness, without city planners batting an eye at the exorbitant values attached to the central motive – high-rent, long-lease commercial real estate. Publicness received, in return for public money, corporate pseudo-public space. The model was deemed successful insofar that it revived post-industrial urban landscape and infrastructure through capital-intensive, public-private redevelopment and initiated new construction of so-called public parks, streets, waterfronts and plazas.

In Prague, the historical core of the city draws millions upon millions of tourists a year. The experience of the city is categorically conditioned by this influx. Parks and squares are swamped by the flow of pedestrians and vehicles. New Prague architecture is strictly determined by the values of this everydayness. Restoration of monuments and gardens is carried out with the implicit intention of appropriation by impassability. The impassable nature of Prague is a sign of its success as a cultural monument – *en masse* – and new architecture and landscape architecture become essentially impassable by necessity. The flow of tourists (which in its most abstract instantiation equals the flow of capital or foreign currency) and the impassability of the streets, squares and parks is in itself the present everyday experience of Prague.

[31] HÉLÈNE CIXOUS, "ATTACKS ON THE CASTLE", ARCHITECTURE AND REVOLUTION, ED. NEIL LEACH, (NEW YORK: ROUTLEDGE, 1999), PP. 228–33

Present-day-planning initiatives in both New York and Prague often are disoriented by the exceptional – in the form of concrete design proposals and, in turn, stymied by the heterogeneous. New parks and cultural facilities planned for formerly benighted regions of both cities attest to the power of the paradigmatic everydayness that destroys difference. The new planetarium for the American Museum of Natural History on the Upper West Side of Manhattan is truly exceptional, but it is dwarfed by concurrent developments under way at Times' Square, where a peculiar corporate heterogeneity is taking root – sub-paradigmatic 'fake' heterogeneity. The historic chaos of Times' Square is in the process of being converted to a carefully orchestrated pseudo-chaos. Independent Broadway theater companies, not to mention the classic seediness of the area have virtually vanished in the face of blockbuster musical productions, mega-stores, high-rise and *de luxe* hotels and office towers and studios for traditional and new media. Prague's Fred-and-Ginger Building (designed by Frank Gehry and Vlado Milunic) remains scandalous today – several years after its completion – because of its *self-conscious* iconic and dissociative form. It refuses to be assimilated. The new Angel City project of Jean Nouvel in Smichov, an industrial and working-class neighborhood of Prague, has raised eyebrows for similar reasons. The iconography and material form of the proposed complex has, however, endured criticism for ten years and Angel City will originate as an exceptional project outside the everydayness of Prague to be in time accepted and part of that everydayness. The highly exceptional Gehry-Milunich building will continue to stand at the outside until the paradigmatic everydayness of Prague shifts toward the heterogeneous (its secret heritage).

Perhaps in acknowledgement of this deficit, New York City's Planning Commissioner has recently proposed changes to the zoning ordinance to allow for buildings of "exceptional design" to violate normative aesthetic and functional restrictions. The justification of "exceptional" status no doubt will be formulated by academic and institutional authorities – e.g. Museum of Modern Art curators and Columbia University professors – with public review kept to a minimum. The proposal to alter the laws governing New York City development has spawned a predictable reaction and the architectural community has aligned itself with the arbiters of avant-garde taste. The argument is that if exceptional aesthetic claims may be made to protect architectural monuments – through landmark designation – then the same claims might be used to breach the restrictive building codes and foster a new era of innovation.[32] This process has played itself out in Prague in a more democratic fashion with the acrimonious debate surrounding the Gehry-Milunic project settled by public referendum.

Landscape in New York and Prague generally suffers the same process of leveling-down. Numerous entries in the 1998 Van Alen Institute East River Competition clearly struck a nerve in the body politic by expropriating former industrial areas along New York's East River for ecological and – simultaneously – recreational purposes. The normative real estate values of city planning were missing from most of the premiated projects. Berlin architect Dagmar Richter's project implanted riparian zones beyond the bulkhead and facilities for purifying the water of the East River. Most of the prize-winning proposals totally rejected the premise that public space must be subsidized by (sold to) public-private development consortiums. Prague's newest park, planned for Prague Castle, is an equally unorthodox treatment of a potentially valuable piece of real estate. The Pheasant's Field site will be converted to a pastoral environment loosely configured in a thematic series of rooms and zones reminiscent of Parc André Citroën in Paris. These rooms will be associated with pavilions programmed to provide minimal amenities to the public. This green zone within the highly regimented castle precinct will, in turn, be countered by a more wild passage through the Hart's 'moat', where no structures whatsoever will be added save an exit footbridge and a tunnel through the obstructing causeway currently bisecting the ravine. Water is being restored via Renaissance irrigation channels to reanimate Pheasant's Field and the moat.

RE-WRITING THE LANGUAGE OF THE WORLD

The public mood everywhere seems to be shifting and this is the case for everydayness saving itself from itself at every opportunity. Landscape, as the quintessential form of conjugating things-in-themselves, is a strategic site for rewriting and collectively re-authorizing the language of the world. The chains of signification that constitute everydayness – the veil described above – are the trappings of charmed environments. Whether

[32] "PLATFORM", DIGITAL DILEMMA (NEW YORK: VAN ALEN INSTITUTE, 1999)

[33] AGAMBEN, INFANCY & HISTORY, P.139

the veil pictures justice or injustice, freedom or enslavement, is the only abstract, formal question to be asked. Beauty, as always, is in the eye – the gaze – of the beholder.

Landscape architecture, in its highest modality, might be conceived as a series of gestures that seeks to revivify entropic states. In transcending the implicit fixity of images landscape might also decompose the modern conception of time: "For in every image there is always a kind of *ligatio* at work, a power that paralyzes, whose spell needs to be broken; it is as if, from the whole history of art, a mute invocation were raised towards the freeing of the image in gesture. This much was expressed in those Greek legends about statues breaking the fetters that contain them and beginning to move; but it is also the intention that philosophy entrusts to the idea, which is not at all – as it is commonly interpreted – a static archetype, but rather a constellation in which phenomena are composed in a gesture."[33] An ecological continuum of socially significant signs – gestures – and the interdependence of natural and cultural systems is the foundation of landscape ethics. Intelligible and sensible orders coincide in the 'symphonic' articulation of generative forms – constellations – constructed at the leading edge of discourse, in the semantic wilderness. This is the true origin of the statement "in wildness is the preservation of the world". This also implies an inversion of linear time and the turning of positivism on its head. As signifying chains, the language of built landscape – urban and otherwise – legitimizes the concept that, in the absence of direct knowledge of the world, the human condition is forged in the interstitial zone between what is (wakefulness) and what might be (desire). The compensatory nature of desire in fact may have a life of its own, but it is built on top of life itself. A chaotic world view may, after all is said and done, be the closest approach possible to the Real, both as a map of subjectivity and a symbolic rite of passage to the coming philosophy – that state of being that will mirror the charmed systems that have produced the world.

CULTURAL ECOLOGY

Andropogon Associates has developed sustainable design methodologies as the central concern of the studio. The principals of Andropogon Associates are the intellectual heirs of the Ian McHarg era at the University of Pennsylvania Department of Landscape Architecture and Regional Planning. Rolf and Leslie Sauer, Carol and Colin Franklin developed process-oriented design with an emphasis on participatory planning and an early role in site selection, program and design of buildings for the landscape architect. The studio combines architecture and land-planning strategies that are a fusion of philosophical and environmental precepts forged in the heady days of late 1960s and 1970s social and ecological activism. Often perceived as weak by artistic standards, sustainable design privileges the ethical nature of subtle and long-term methodologies versus the whims of imposed, structurally aggressive formal and synthetic landscape types. The struggle of the 'Real' versus the 'Big Other' is played out (although in terms unfamiliar to Lacanian psychoanalysis).

Andropogon has specifically pursued alternative technologies for dealing with storm water drainage, the bugaboo of landscape design and usually relegated to a civil engineer and dealt with in a purely mechanical way. The subsurface groundwater recharge systems developed by Andropogon, increasingly required by city and regional planning agencies, originated with a critique of the ready-made systems of containment and dispersal used in urban and suburban America for the past 100 years. Channeling storm water off site, into rivers and marshes, typically led to the lowering of the water table in the immediate environs of inhabited lands as well as the contamination of wetlands. This led, over time, to the reduction of biodiversity and the conversion of developed landscape to high-maintenance, energy-consumptive gardens, parks and parkways.

Andropogon has used porous paving and subsurface leaching beds as a means of returning water that runs off paved surfaces to the local water table. The development of naturalistic ponds and streams in campus-style landscape also has become a standard form of storing and conserving rainwater. Much of Andropogon's work from the 1970s has been absorbed into common practice in the 1990s.

Algonquin Gas Transmission Corridor – the Indian name is particularly picturesque and representative of colloquial place names subsumed by corporate America – was developed by removing large chunks of the forest floor with a modified front-end loader. The roots and rhizomes were stockpiled during excavation, *in situ* welding and burial of the pipeline and returned to the woodland corridor as ready-made landscape. This same stripping technique has been utilized by landscape architect A. E. Bye to provide instant 'landscape' to newly forged residential properties in the woodlands of New England. In the Algonquin Corridor, the forest 'sod' was replaced and a new path system traces the winding route of the underground pipeline through the forest (providing both a *de facto* maintenance road and an easy surface to excavate should the pipeline need replacement or repair). This conservation methodology, commonly referred to as "mitigation", typically involves the creation of a simulated landscape elsewhere in exchange for destroying an authentic one somewhere. Andropogon seems interested instead in putting back as much of the 'authentic' landscape as possible. But this is not always possible, and in the highly charged debates concerning environmental restoration, mitigation has begun to assume distinctive 'negative' connotations with purists who consider it a deal with the devil.

Both the Passaic River greenbelt and the Delaware River tidal wetland are examples of current wholesale reclamation projects under-way in regionally significant waterways and wetlands. Federal laws – and the Army Corps of Engineers – have begun to reverse decades of warfare waged over controlling rivers and flood basins. Massive federal subsidies have been applied to restoring natural outflows and native plant systems to both polluted and ravaged wetland environments. These projects involve stabilizing plant communities and removing artificial dikes and barriers to allow water to move 'as it pleases' and to encourage the return of natural homeostatic processes and re-colonization by interdependent species. Often these projects involve providing controlled public access and the structures inserted into the riparian zones are minimal – simple, rustic and unobtrusive walkways, bridges and piers. Linear greenways are a particularly 'pregnant' outcome of the de-industrialization of American waterways and waterfronts. This on-going process of

121

122

123

reclamation represents an historical irony – the broad brush of the environmental planner and landscape architect is now enlisted to counter the *ad hoc* instrumentalism of architect-engineers from industrial era America.

Andropogon has defied the usual narrow field of operations for the landscape architect by entering the planning and programming aspects of design projects at the opening stages and steering the conceptual and organizational apparatus of the client brief toward a more highly integrated program placing environmental and interpretive integrity first. This approach naturally limits the type of projects undertaken by the studio to those with implicit ecological and cultural principles. Perhaps the most striking component of this enhanced role for the landscape architect is the placement or siting of buildings versus the more standard role of helping to reintegrate the architecture with the environment after the site plan has been established.

121 | 122
Godfrey Pond,
Villanova, PA,
before and after work

123
Delaware River,
tidal wetland

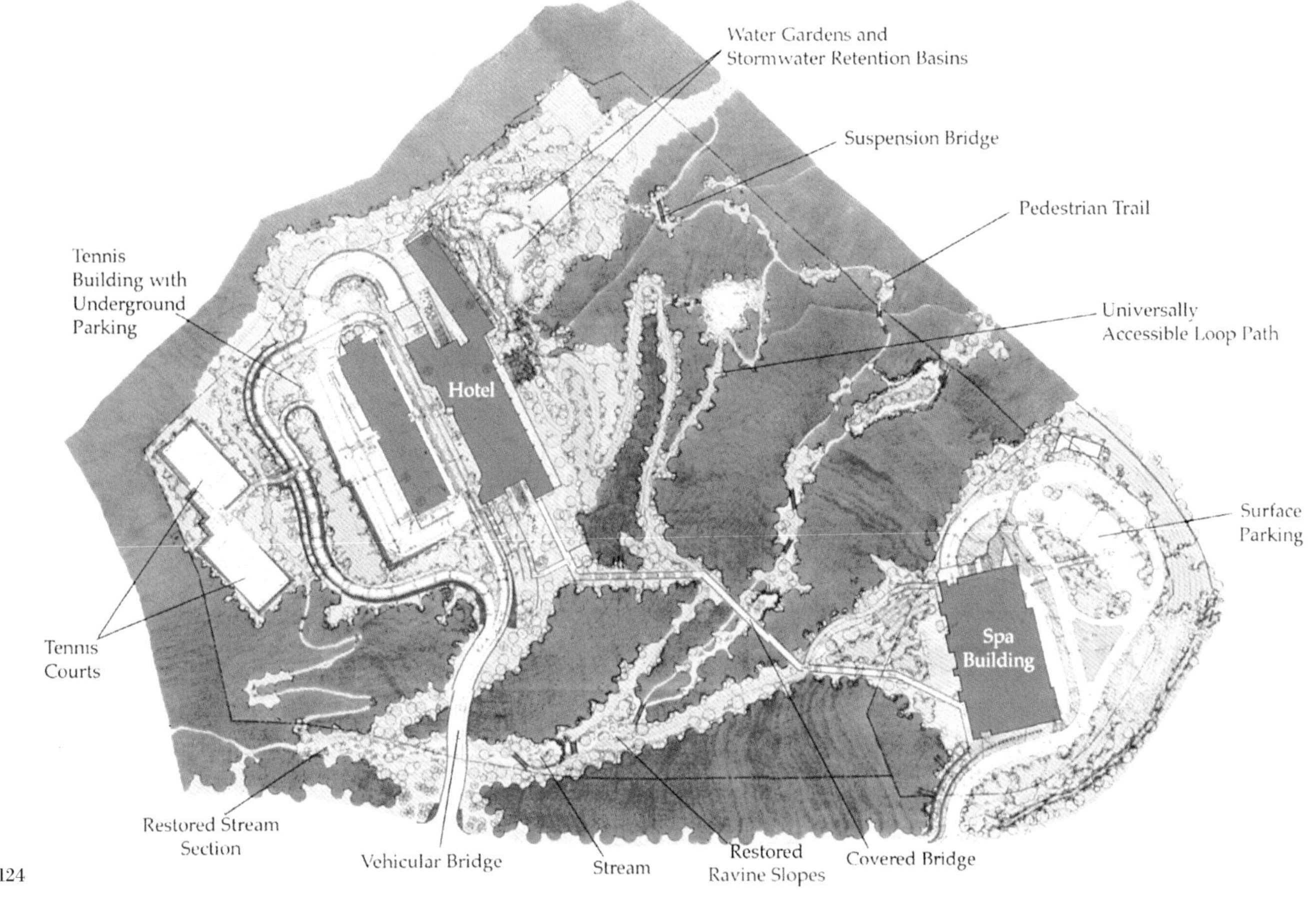

124

NIKKO KIRIFURI RESORT — NIKKO CITY, JAPAN WITH VENTURI, SCOTT BROWN & ASSOCIATES

Nikko Kirifuri Resort was commissioned by the Japanese Ministry of Ports and Telecommunications and is adjacent to Nikko National Park, "a site of ancient Buddhist and Shinto shrines". Its hotel and spa culture required a close integration of facilities with the natural environment. Small and compact, its invisible borders enclose no more than 35 acres. The complex includes a 97-room hotel, a conference center, tennis courts, spa and swimming facilities. Situated in mountainous and wooded territory, the topography was naturally given to selective editing and classic gardening stratagems such as 'hide and seek' and 'borrowed landscape'. The elongated building forms trace the natural plateau at the 941–950-ft. contours of the site, stepping up the hill in a coordinated and organic fashion. The site plan exploits the natural tableau of the flattened hillside, perching the main facilities above the ravines and cascading streams.

124
Nikko Kirifuri Resort, Nikko City, Japan, site plan

125 | 126

127

128

129

130

131

Andropogon utilized many of their signature land reclamation methodologies including the channeling and manipulation of storm water. In this case the steep topography required stone and vegetative reinforcement of these channels to prevent erosion. The latter was accomplished using willow species (Salix) that have highly ramified root systems that slow and filter moving water as well as hidden, sub-grade concrete steps – a necessary supplement, but pure artifice. Three linked ornamental ponds effectively channel and disperse the rainwater from the roof and paved surfaces of the complex. These ponds are all conceived as living systems with plant, insect, animal and micro-organic life forms re-introduced and supplemented.

Venturi, Scott Brown designed the main bridge as an "imageful sign" and a practical measure spanning the 150-meter-wide gorge; it is turned perpendicular to the approach road for maximum exposure to the gaze of approaching visitors. The architecture is based on traditional rural Japanese forms and, like most Robert Venturi projects, is a "scenographic architecture" with overt simplifications of the referenced building forms overlaid with decorative appliqués. Especially the entrance drive, once it reaches the hotel, is significant by its curious contrast to the wild site. The clean edges and the urban street form present the image of a civilized enclave in a 'primitive' setting. This image belies the history of the site uncovered by Andropogon – the deposition of volcanic ash created a forest type heavily exploited by Japanese industries. A probable clear-cutting of the site toward the end of the Second World War for timber was indicated by the fact that all extant trees on the site were no more than 50 years old.

Andropogon was responsible for restoring the site after construction and accomplished this feat by removing and storing in a rice paddy nursery most of the local, indigenous plants in the way of construction. Temporary access roads were removed and re-vegetated after completion of the complex. 40 percent of the plantings were from salvaged trees and shrubs. The planting palette was conceived as a gradient moving from horticultural to wild species as the areas surrounding the hotel merged with the range of habitats of the lower and upper forest.

125
Nikko Kirifuri, cantilevered bridge over gorge

126
Nikko Kirifuri, misted entrance drive

127
Nikko Kirifuri, rising woodland path

128
Nikko Kirifuri, zig-zag woodland path

129
Nikko Kirifuri, lower ponds

130
Nikko Kirifuri, waterfall storm water system

131
Nikko Kirifuri, rope suspension footbridge

The arboretum is situated in the historic Chestnut Hill area of Philadelphia and functions as both a research facility and an amenity landscape. As in England, the great estates of the American East Coast have slowly fallen to public or institutional management and serve as *de facto* bio-reserves in both suburban and metropolitan environments. The Morris estate was ceded to the University of Pennsylvania in 1933. Like art historian Bernard Berenson's (1865–1959) 16th-century Villa I Tatti (in Florence, Italy), now a satellite of Harvard University, the Morris Arboretum contains mnemonic *fabriqué* – follies – and classicizing gardens typical of Renaissance Romantic Classicism. Romantic Classicism, a synchronic humanist mindset reappearing in time as a cultural phoenix, was transplanted to late-19th and early-20th century America by way of English-style landscape gardening.

A long-term vision for the 175-acre arboretum, the master plan includes threading roadways through the 1887 Victorian-era estate and the conversion of the historic property to a public facility. The public areas of the arboretum comprise 92 acres with the land divided into "symbolic", "natural", "park" and "working" zones. The mission of the arboretum is to integrate art, science and the humanities through cultural programs sponsored by the University of Pennsylvania.

The entrance road winds through the Wissahickon floodplain passing through representative landscape types – meadows, woodland, working farm – and terminating at the hilltop where the demolished mansion and period formal gardens stood. The extant carriage house was converted to serve as visitor amenities in absence of the mansion. The main portion of the estate is an informal collection of botanic specimens and gardens spread over the park environment. This Victorian mishmash – the collector's garden – has been slowly reordered to open the meadows and vistas of the pastoral tableau and concentrate the horticultural elements in garden rooms. Andropogon's role – as stewards of the long-term plan initiated in 1978 – has centered on the design and siting of the wandering entry road, the provision of parking bays near the visitors center, the creation of a circuit of paths and walks throughout the 92-acre public sector and the restructuring of the plantings. The road and parking grove collect and channel rainwater into the local landscape through a porous paving and subterranean leaching system developed with Cahill Associates.

132
Morris Arboretum, Philadelphia, PA, meadow and entrance drive

133
Morris Arboretum, site plan

132

133

134

135

136

137

134
Morris Arboretum, parking grove with porous surface (left)

135
Morris Arboretum, watercolor painting of entrance drive and carriage house

136 | 137
Morris Arboretum, gardens and greenhouses

138

CROSBY ARBORETUM – PICAYUNE

Located in the Pearl River Basin of Mississippi, the 640-acre Crosby Arboretum is an educational center for the study of the interrelation of natural and human systems. The arboretum is surrounded by an additional reserve of nearly 1000 acres of coastal plain habitat. The main visitor area – Piney Woods Lake – is a lowland marsh created in an area once used for the cultivation of strawberries. The habitat is an imaginary take on what might have existed and was created by extensive excavation and subsequent flooding. Boardwalks permit visitors to wander through the marsh among the indigenous gum and cypress trees.

The surrounding pinewood – a mix of loblolly and slash pine – has been retained as the backdrop for this artificial or 'naturalistic' wetland. Pinecot Pavilion, designed by architect Fay Jones (Jones & Jennings, Fayetteville, Arkansas), dominates the lakefront with its dramatic wood-frame construction and open-joist tracery. The pine woodland comprises 30 acres and is representative of the North American Gulf Coast ecosystem. A savanna – meadow with widely scattered trees and colonized by grasses and wildflowers – is managed by prescribed burning. Human systems are overtly represented in building forms both completed and planned – but also in the patently invented ecology of the site and the management regime of selective coercion.

The ecological 'mapping' process utilized by Andropogon identified plant habitats based on two interrelated gradients: a time-based succession and a moisture-based system of species distribution and diversification. Andropogon sited all architectural structures and introduced the four-fold path system – the path loop, the lake path, the long path and the forest path – while progressively replanting the areas of the arboretum with whole plant communities versus plant specimens.

138
Crosby Arboretum, Picayune, MS, bird's-eye view of site excavation and pavilion construction

139 | 140

141

139
Crosby Arboretum, flooded site and pavilion

140
Crosby Arboretum, pedestrian bridge and pavilion

141
Crosby Arboretum, dry meadow

ANDROPOGON ASSOCIATES, LTD | 374 SHURS LANE | PHILADELPHIA, PA 19128
T 215 487 0700 | F 215 483 7520

ANDROPOGON ASSOCIATES was formed in 1975 to bring an ecological perspective to problem solving in landscape architecture. The work encompasses all the traditional areas of environmental planning and design as well as a number of emerging specialties. The firm has established ties to the academic and scientific communities and is multi-disciplinary. It works from a consensus-building model of planning, from the early stages of project conception through construction management. Its areas of specialty include adaptive reuse and restoration of natural, historical and degraded landscapes in a wide range of contexts. Andropogon's founding partners – Rolf and Leslie Sauer, Carol and Colin Franklin – all trained at the University of Pennsylvania Graduate School of Design under Ian McHarg.

SELECTED PROJECTS

National Storytelling Center
Jonesborough, TN, built 2000

Trexler Memorial Park
Allentown, PA, design 1996

Nikko Kirifuri Resort
(w/ Venturi, Scott Brown), Nikko City, Japan, built 1995

Stapleton Master Plan
Denver, CO, design 1995

Louisville Olmsted Parks
Louisville, KY, design 1992-present

Central Park Woodlands
New York City, NY, design 1990

Crosby Arboretum
Picayune, MS, built 1989

SmithKline Beecham Agricultural Products Headquarters
1987

Morris Arboretum of the University of Pennsylvania
Philadelphia, PA, design 1975-present

University of Pennsylvania Master Plan & Phased Projects
Philadelphia, PA, design 1976-present

SELECTED BIBLIOGRAPHY

PAUL BENNETT, "The Other Side of the Fence: What Drives Landscape Architecture Now"
Architectural Record (January 2000)

PAUL BENNETT, "Ecologizing Olmsted"
[Iroquois Park, Louisville, KY], Landscape Architecture (June 1998)

CAROL FRANKLIN, "Fostering Living Landscapes"
George F. Thompson and Frederick R. Steiner, editors, Ecological Design and Planning (New York: John Wiley & Sons, 1997)

FREDERICK STEINER AND TODD JOHNSON, "Fitness, Adaptability, Delight"
Landscape Architecture (March 1990)

LESLIE SAUER, "The North Woods of Central Park"
Landscape Architecture (March 1993)

"Mielparque Nikko Kirifuri Resort, Nikko National Park
Japan, "1992–1997", Zodiac (January-June 1999)

"Venturi, Scott Brown and Associates: 1990s Works"
[Nikko Kirifuri], Space Design (August 1997)

"Unterhaltungsmilieus"
Werk, Bauen + Wohnen (April 1998)

"Andropogon: The Restoration of Nature"
Design Book Review (Spring 1991)

"Healing Central Park's Woodlands"
Landscape Architecture (August 1989)

142
Crosby Arboretum, moist meadow

143
Crosby Arboretum, gravel road

144
Crosby Arboretum, prescribed burn of savanna

145
Crosby Arboretum, aquatic zone

142 | 143

109

ANDROPOGON ASSOCIATES — PHILADELPHIA

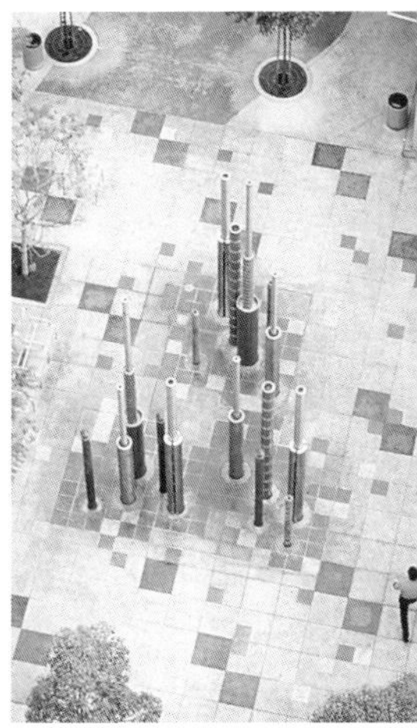
146

BURTON & COMPANY – SANTA MONICA

HELIOTROPIC HETEROTOPIAS

For 25 years Pamela Burton and Company has provided landscape architectural and planning services to clients in the Los Angeles area and beyond. These projects are primarily institutional and public landscapes that combine interest in fine-textured urbanism and synoptic natural environments. Informed by history, literature and ecology, Burton and Company projects have a 'high' horticultural sensibility that enhances the structural logic of the design by adding symbolic and cultural significance.

Los Angeles is famously a place of extremes, both environmental and social. The economic and cultural gaps between rich and poor are expressed in the aesthetic distance between the micro-texture of downtown Los Angeles and the luxuriant green enclaves north and west of the City – north of Wilshire Boulevard. But this divide is also expressed in the actual physical structure of Los Angeles. Situated within the scenic topographic diversity of the Santa Monica-San Gabriel geologic rift – and pictured in the elite enclaves of Bel Air, Beverly Hills, Brentwood, Pacific Palisades, and Malibu – the privileged zones 'above' the City are mediated by reliance on the automobile and the extensive freeway system of coastal California.

Burton and Company instrumentalize this physical and sociological chasm as a means of inserting public landscape within the fractured social topography. Los Liones Park, in Pacific Palisades, is but a portion of a vast trail system above the City and open to public recreation. It is also a transitional area between the leafy Palisades community and high Topanga State Park, a rugged site for hiking and strolling. The Los Liones master plan (1993) acknowledges the presence of riparian zones within the park and seeks to restore the hydrological integrity of the basin in direct contrast

146
Biddy Mason Park, Los Angeles, CA, sculpture

147
Biddy Mason Park, location plan

148|149
Los Liones Park, Pacific Palisades, CA, trails

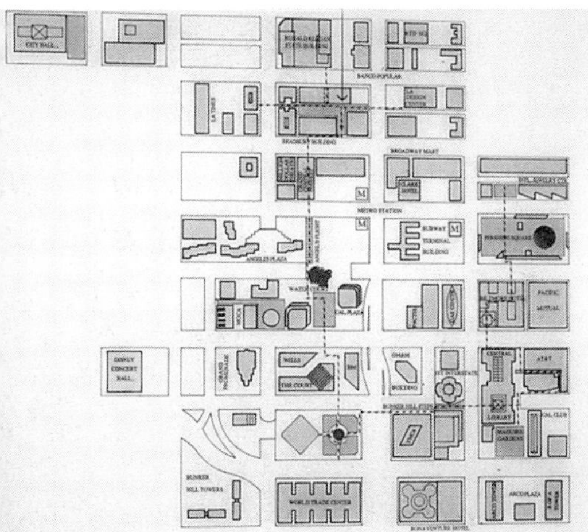

147

to the long-standing canalization and evacuation of storm water in the Los Angeles plain. Famously, the Los Angeles River is now a concrete ditch running straight to the Pacific. It has even been suggested that it might be used as a seasonal freeway, during the dry season.

On the other end of the scale, in terms of location and function, Burton and Company's Biddy Mason Park (1991) is a 'vest pocket' park shoe-horned between existing buildings in the historic Broadway district of downtown Los Angeles. Part of a now defunct CRA (Commercial Recreation Area) plan for the mostly Hispanic area near Grand Central Market, the park commemorates an African-American 19th-century midwife – Biddy Mason – born into slavery but freed in the late 1800s. The plan for the plaza respects the Los Angeles grid while providing respite from the utilitarian sameness of the surrounding blocks with a fountain and pathway flanked by Jacaranda trees. A sculptural fountain fabricated from metal piping is emblematic of the oil drilling and refining legacy of the City. The park is conceived as an "archetypal court and grove" befitting the 'mediterranean' climate of Los Angeles. The memorial wall, designed by Dolores Hayden and Sheila De Brettville, contributes historic value to the formal composition.

148

149

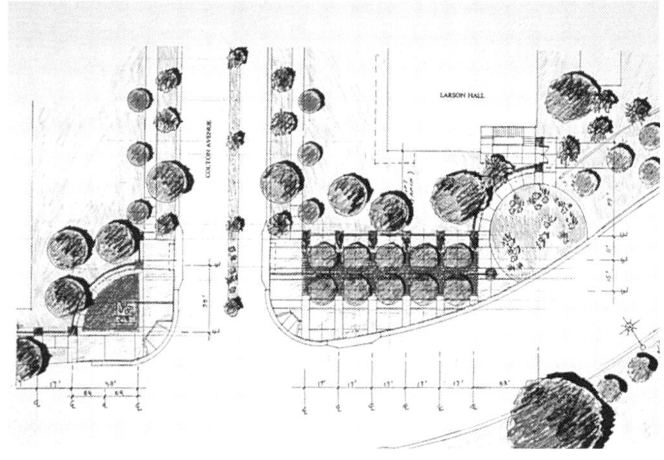

150

151

COLTON AVENUE — REDLANDS WITH MEYER AND ALLEN ASSOCIATES

Burton's Colton Avenue project embodies the 'classic' concept of gateway – in this case for the 1909 neo-classical University of Redlands campus – without adopting a self-conscious architectural *mise-en-scène* methodology. Charles Moore's Beverly Hills Civic Center and the gateway to San Francisco's Chinatown are but two examples of the fabulous, sometimes monstrous implications of this typology. Instead, Burton and Company, working with Meyer and Allen Associates, introduce landscape forms that form the essential fabric of the experience while appropriating extant infrastructure. A typical southern California open storm drain – constructed of decomposed granite and populated by granite 'erratics' – is outfitted with grasses and succulents and framed with Mexican Fan Palms. Architectural gateways in fact are included but formulated in a demure fashion and cloaked in Wisteria. Avenues leading to the campus are tree-lined and intended to formalize the quaint Spanish 'mediterranean' texture of the Redlands campus.

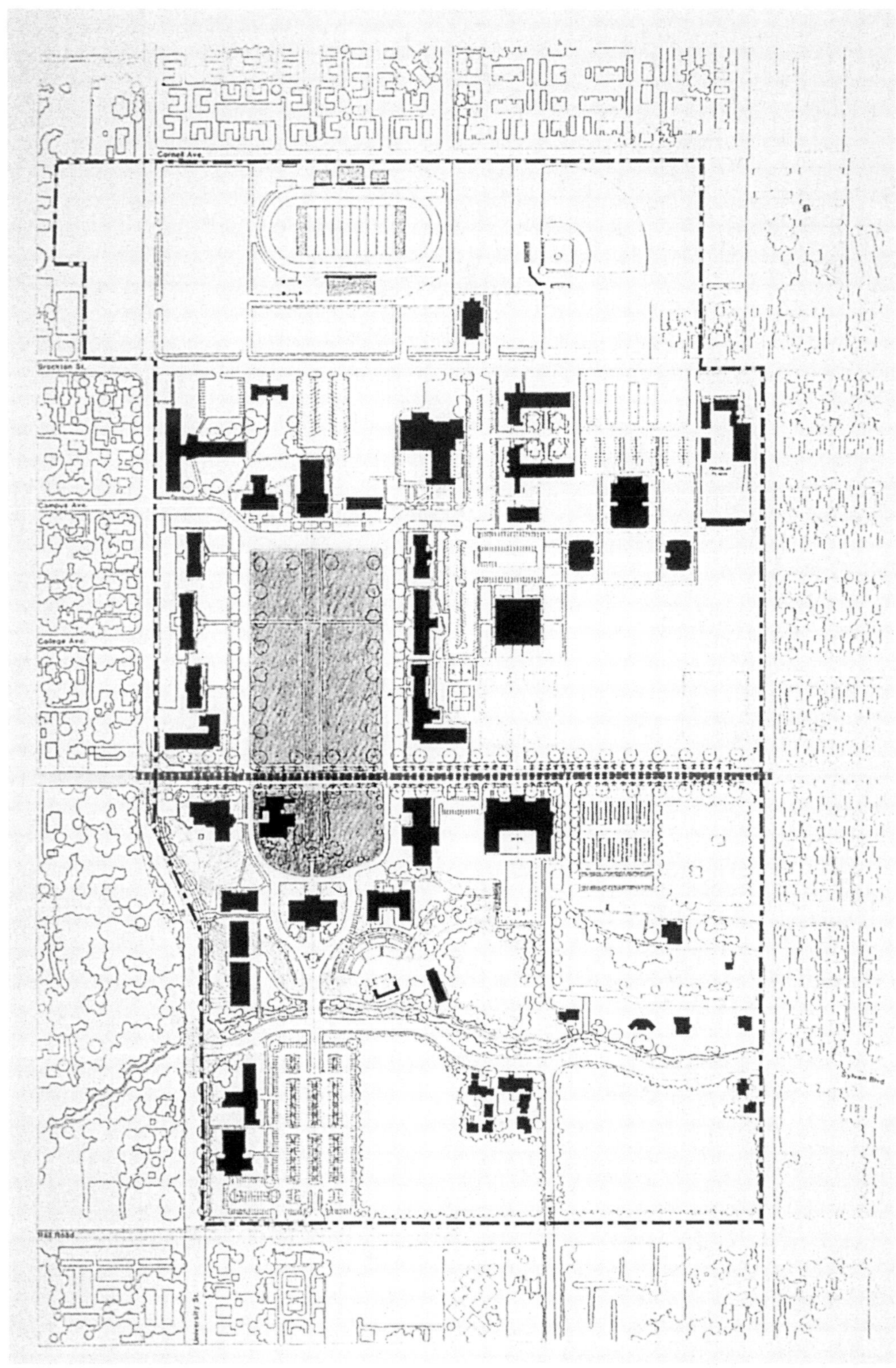

152

150
Colton Avenue,
University of Redlands,
Redlands, CA,
detail of planting plan

151
Colton Avenue,
vegetated storm drain and
view of 'campanile'

152
Colton Avenue,
campus plan

153

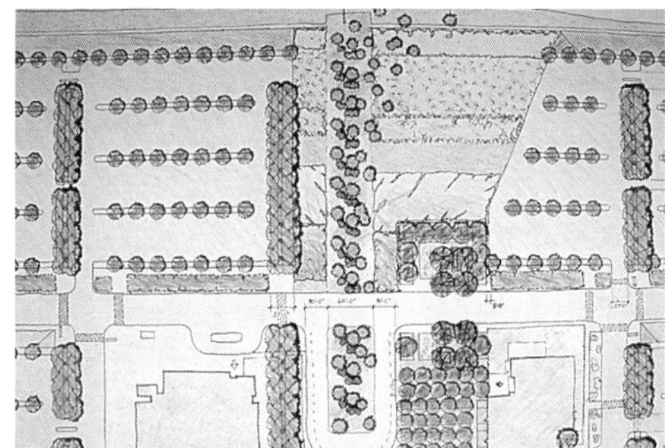

154

HIGH DESERT MEDICAL CENTER — LANCASTER WITH ANSHEN + ALLEN AND VILLANUEVA ARNONI ARCHITECTS

High Desert Medical Center was designed to stand in now suburban land first colonized in the 19th century. The project utilizes the geometric organizational *parti* of California's agricultural lands while integrating garden environments within the armatures of a hospital complex. Blended hedgerows of tall dense trees normally used in agricultural windbreaks are included. The trees serve as an organizational device for orientation within the vast parking lot while providing shelter from wind and sun. The xeric soil conditions and the presence of high winds and cool night-time temperatures required that the broad structural order be subdivided to create microclimatic regions within the armature of the building mass. This area, known as the Central Garden, is an extension of the primary care facilities of the hospital. It is comprised of a series of healing gardens linked by a walkway and demarcated by paired Stone Pines. Protection from climatic extremes is supplied by the massing of trees in a north-south direction and through orientation of the building to create opportunities to maximize courtyards and passages for public outdoor gardens and groves. The planting of lawns and ornamental shrubberies contradicts the local climatic conditions and requires ample water resources for maintenance but is nonetheless consistent with the Californian trend to irrigate otherwise marginal landscape for the production of artificial oases.

153
High Desert Medical Center, Lancaster, CA, model of campus

154
High Desert Medical Center, vehicular circulation and planting plan

155
High Desert Medical Center, perspective sketch of gardens

156
High Desert Medical Center, wind berm study

155

156

157

158

157
High Desert Medical Center, poplar windbreak

158
High Desert Medical Center, eucalyptus windbreak and citrus grove typology

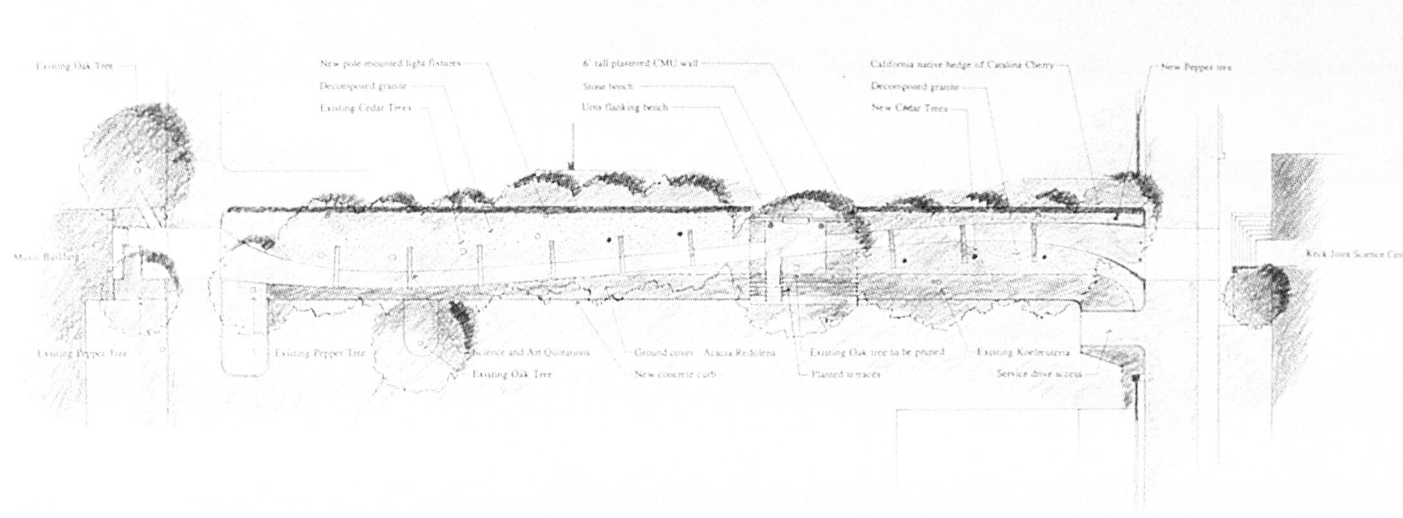

159

QUOTATIONS WALK — CLAREMONT

A modest example of 'writing' in the landscape, Quotations Walk – at Scripps College – incorporates 9 literary citations dispersed along a walkway leading from the Music Building at the Fine Arts Complex to the Keck Joint Science Center at the far corner of the campus. The mnemonic, literary stroll is interrupted with a stepped garden room shaded by a mature Coast Live Oak. The room is framed by a section of wall meant to imply an historic fragment – it is based on the Kauffman and Trout architectural language of the campus – and copies of c. 1925 blue urns (designed by Gladding McBean) lend an 'archaeological' ambience to the tableau. Plato's Academy is inferred – but indirectly and through elision versus self-conscious quotation.

160

161

162

PAMELA BURTON & COMPANY | 2324 MICHIGAN AVENUE | SANTA MONICA, CA 90404
T 310 828 6373 | F 310 828 8054
burtonco@aol.com

PAMELA BURTON & COMPANY is a Santa Monica-based landscape architecture firm established in 1975. The office specializes in urban design and master-planning work for institutional, commercial and civic clients. The firm also works at the residential scale creating garden oases with a strong regional ambiance. Projects combine an unusually fluid sense of historical, horticultural and symbolic expertise that is underwritten by a sense of 'rooted-ness' in the mediterranean climate of Southern California. Local geography, ecology and cultural history are synthesized in projects that defy normal classification and, instead, exude a classic aura of atonement and reconciliation.

SELECTED PROJECTS

Santa Monica/UCLA Hospital
Santa Monica, CA, in construction, 2005

Farmer's Market
Los Angeles, CA, in construction 2000

Gilbert Residence
Los Angeles, CA, built 1999

Colton Avenue
Redlands, CA, built 1997

Scripps College Quotations Walk
Millard Sheets Art Center, Founder's Court, Keck Joint Science Center, Claremont, CA, built 1995

Chiate Residence
Malibu, CA, built 1995

California Center for the Arts
Escondido, CA, built 1994

Moore Residence
Malibu, CA, built 1994

Los Liones Park Masterplan
Pacific Palisades, CA, built 1993

High Desert Hospital
Lancaster, CA, design 1992

University of California
Clinical Sciences Building, Science and Engineering Research Facility, Classroom Building, San Diego (La Jolla), CA, built 1991

Biddy Mason Park
Los Angeles, CA, built 1991

SELECTED BIBLIOGRAPHY

PAMELA BURTON, "Urban Revisions: Current Projects for the Public Realm"
[MOCA, Los Angeles exhibition review], Landscape Journal (Spring 1995)

PAMELA BURTON AND RICHARD HERTZ, "Healing and Cultivation"
Modulus 20 (1991)

PAMELA BURTON AND RICHARD HERTZ, "Language of Scripted Spaces"
Landscape Review (1996)

PAMELA BURTON, "The Land Cannot Be Measured"
Margaret Reeve and Michael Rotondi (eds.), Design Process @ Sci-Arc (New York: Monacelli Press, 1997)

PAMELA BURTON, "Firestorms: Re-ordering California Landscapes"
Landscape Australia 1994 Garden Design Conference (March 1994)

JANE BROWN GILLETTE, "Great Performances"
[Escondido], Landscape Architecture (March 1996)

JOHN DIXON HUNT, "Arcadia"
Landscape Journal (Spring 1996)

MATTHEW POTTEIGER AND JAMIE PURINTON, Landscape Narratives: Design Practices for Story Telling
(New York: John Wiley & Sons, 1998)

HEATH SCHENKER, "Language of Scripted Spaces"
Landscape Journal (1995)

NORIYOSHI SUZUKI, "Pamela Burton"
CASA-Brutus (Spring-Summer 1997)

JAMES GRAYSON TRULOVE, "The New American Garden: Innovations in Residential Landscape Architecture"
(New York: Whitney Library of Design, 1998)

"Transforming the American Garden: 12 New Landscape Designs"
[Exhibition review], Places (Special Issue 1986)

"Kennedy Marshall Residence"
GA Houses 54 (November 1997)

"Place of Privilege"
Places (Summer 1994)

"Landscape Design: New Wave in California"
Process Architecture (Tokyo: Bunji Murotani, 1985)

"Metaphor + Ritual: Contemporary Landscape Projects"
arts+architecture (Fall 1982)

159
Quotations Walk, Scripps College, Claremont, CA, plan

160
Quotations Walk, terraces with urns

161|162
Quotations Walk, inscriptions

163

ANDREW SPURLOCK MARTIN POIRIER – SAN DIEGO

PRACTICAL REASON

Andrew Spurlock and Martin Poirier are design chameleons – a perhaps apt simile for work based in Southern California. The studio's projects span large-scale planning studies to site-specific installations that reveal an artistic ideal attuned to public art and public open space. Sensitive to urban context, they have collaboratively designed small-scale urban housing – an idiom often marked by neo-conservative or new urbanist fantasy versus community-based intertextuality – working with a small group of regional architects. Some of these same regionalists – valorized in Kenneth Frampton's critique of "critical regionalism" – in the late 1980s jumped ship and formed the Congress for New Urbanism effectively overwriting idiomatic regional design vocabularies with a more ideological anti-modern rhetoric.

Spurlock Poirier is concerned with 'character' – qualities in and of existing places – that transcends the borrowed identities typical of classic urbanism and picturesque resort planning. Design, according to this perspective, can only reflect an inherent order and beauty. It can never successfully impose a model in spite of local character. Anti-nostalgic, this philosophy of place resists the usual claims of city-beautiful ideology – the reliance on, for 'essence', traditional European cities or historic village enclaves. This realism is the source of design idioms that fly in the face of the suburban-urban divide ruling American urban planning based on zoning and mutually exclusive development models. Acknowledging the vital density of the city, Spurlock Poirier work within the structure of the existing conditions, not to alter that density but to refine and extend its scope and to absorb the implicit segregation encoded in built form in Southern California.

163 | 164
Molecular Biology Research Facility, University of California, San Diego, CA, grove / path and stair

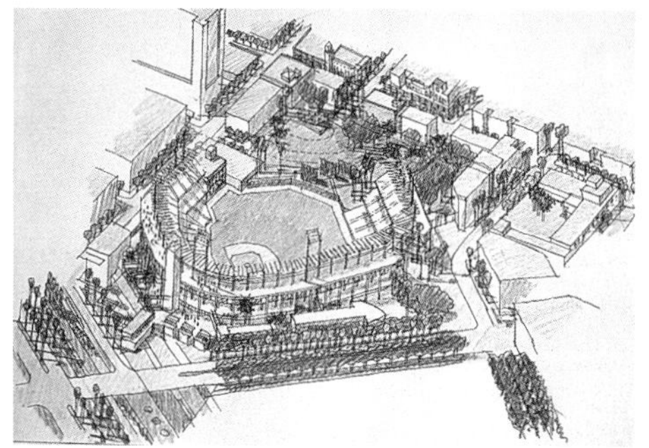

165

166

Collaborative projects with artists – Robert Irwin, Alexis Smith, Jackie Ferrara, Newton and Helen Harrison, Christine Oatman – including the controversial Getty Center Garden – leads the studio into fertile abstract and formal territory but without the turning of their collective backs on the emotional and intellectual currents of community-based design. This process resembles a built version of Jürgen Habermas neo-Enlightenment communicative project restoring practical reason within *de facto* hegemony.

Spurlock Poirier's entry for the West Hollywood Veterans Memorial is an intentionally provocative take on the American billboard. Its form – seen from afar – is to appear as a sign (it is 15-ft. tall and 20-ft. above ground) with ambiguous intent. The blur of metal dog tags and the steel lattice framework at first conceal the significance of the strategic image, a dissembling urban fixture at the bend in Santa Monica Boulevard caused by the southern thrust of the Hollywood Hills. As the boulevard also widens at this point, view corridors to the memorial are enhanced and a focal point for the somewhat polyphonic streetscape is realized. The billboard form is destabilized by lack of narrative content and by more discrete notations embedded in the site only evident by closer personal contact and comprehension. These elements include a water runnel beneath quartzite sandstone, a 4-ft.-high west wall forming an entrance to the park, a hedge and a 5-branch insignia set in sandstone identifying the military memorial as a comprehensive memorial for all branches of service. The most discrete layer of information is contained in the dog tags, submitted by anyone anywhere with 4 military and non-military characteristics of the person commemorated – e.g. country of origin, family heritage or cultural identification, sexual preference, political affiliation, religion, commendations, tours of duty, rank and blood type.

165|166
San Diego Ballpark
with Antoine Predock,
San Diego, CA,
concept sketches

167|168

167|168
West Hollywood Veterans Memorial, Los Angeles, CA, model views

169

170

KETTNER ROW — SAN DIEGO WITH JONATHAN SEGAL ARCHITECT AND ROB WELLINGTON QUIGLEY

Kettner Row, created *ex nihilo* in San Diego's Little Italy between Beech and Cedar streets, is similar in form to strips of traditional row houses populating both east and west coast American cities. The typology is a classic space-saving urban planning device with back lots usually situated along narrow alleys. The project comprises 16 3-story townhouses with units 15-ft.-by-50-ft. in size with a typical back garden-court 15-ft.-by-15-ft. 12 units have rear gardens and 5 include 'granny flats' (2-story apartments).

Back gardens usually offset minimal front gardens, in this centuries old *parti*, and stoops and "English" basements typify the frontality of the model. Entered at the 2nd- or 1st-story level, the row house engages the street through its variable architectonic streetwall and the alternation of roof planes, bays and balconies projecting into the space of the street. At Kettner Row, a more pronounced concatenation of forms updates the uniformity of the traditional row house – a form that predates the modern tract house - and connotes complexity and sociability.

A communal garden, at midblock, is enclosed by the wraparound architectural ensemble. The upper-middle-class enclave is 3 blocks from San Diego Bay in an office, retail and restaurant mixed-use district. The units sold from $190 000 – $290 000 and several are used as live-work spaces.

169
Kettner Row, San Diego, CA, row house facade

170
Kettner Row, twilight, looking north to Helmut Jahn's One America Plaza

171
Kettner Row, site plan

172
Kettner Row, sidewalk and stoops

173
Kettner Row, front garden and stoop

174
Kettner Row, gardens, looking south

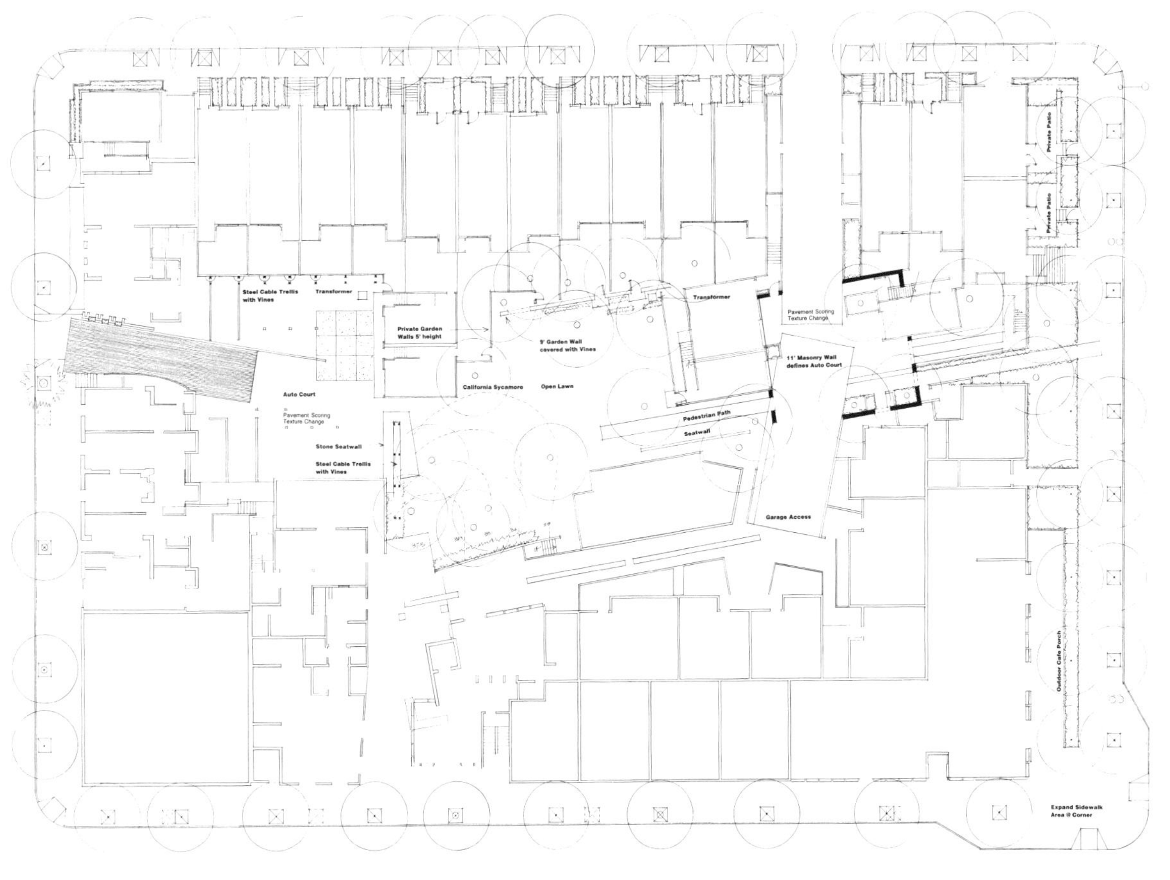

171

172

173

174

175

176

TIJUANA ESTUARY VISITORS CENTER — SAN DIEGO WITH ROB WELLINGTON QUIGLEY

A collaborative project by Rob Wellington Quigley and Land Studio (Andrew Spurlock and partners), Tijuana Estuary Visitors Center is Andrew Spurlock and Land Studio's paean to natural largess at the edge of urbanity.

The project is located at the north edge of the Tijuana River National Estuarine Research Reserve bordering Tijuana, Mexico. The Center serves as a gateway to the coastal tide flats and hills separating San Diego and the Pacific Ocean; it is effectively 'adrift' in the estuarine scrub but within earshot of a single-family residential housing enclave. Surrounded by re-vegetated tidal basins and an educative part of the larger reserve that protects the wetlands associated with the east-west flowing Tijuana River, a demonstration garden near the Center contains 100 species of sage-scrub vegetation.

Sited near Imperial Beach, on state land, the project redefines the edge of the city as a place to both view the City and gainsay the City while touching exiled 'first nature'. A popular hiking and horseback riding area, the beach and trails connect to Borderfield State Park, south of San Diego.

177

178

175
Tijuana Estuary Visitors Center, San Diego, CA, bird's-eye perspective

176
Tijuana Estuary Visitors Center, scrub lands

177
Tijuana Estuary Visitors Center, Visitors Center and San Diego 'skyline'

178
Tijuana Estuary Visitors Center, gardens

126

SNAKE PATH — SAN DIEGO WITH ALEXIS SMITH

The University of California's San Diego campus was reprogrammed as a vast 'sculpture garden' in 1982 with the first installations of the Stuart Collection. Permanent works by international artists – Kiki Smith, Robert Irwin, Ian Hamilton Finlay, Bruce Nauman, Nam June Paik and others – were installed in both the grounds and the campus buildings making figurative links between the educational and natural environs. Overlooking the Pacific Ocean, the 1200-acre campus in the La Jolla district affords dramatic views of the Pacific from the high mesa. It approaches the infinite and the sublime through visually colonizing – like Louis Kahn's nearby Salk Institute – the vast open spaces of the Pacific Ocean.

The 560-ft.-by-10-ft. Snake Path, designed by artist Alexis Smith with technical assistance by Spurlock Poirier, is executed in colored slate tiles – "scales" – and extends through the grounds coiling and encircling the sculptural and garden forms. The serpent links the Central Library and open space reserved for the future Warren Mall. Near its tail, the body of the snake rounds an outsized granite version of Milton's epic poem *Paradise Lost*. Near its head, a tropical "Garden of Eden" is caught in a circular coil as the body of the snake path winds through the eucalyptus groves and chaparral of the campus.

The snake resembles a diamondback rattler, which is of course the telltale denizen – bugaboo – of high desert landscape. In Southern California, essentially desert and chaparral, walking on a rattler is tantamount to riding the tail of a tiger – another metaphor for the pursuit of knowledge. In this case the rattler has been 'domesticated' and poses no direct threat. Its presence, however, implicates the terror associated with wild nature and the unknowable expanses of the American West while – more to the point – picturing the wilderness of knowledge (and information) embodied in a modern university.

179
Snake Path,
University of California,
San Diego, CA,
bird's eye view

180

The Collection

1 Terry Allen *Trees*, 1986
2 Michael Asher *Untitled*, 1992
3 Jackie Ferrara *Terrace*, 1991
4 Ian Hamilton Finlay *UNDA*, 1987
5 Richard Fleischner *La Jolla Project*, 1984
6 Jenny Holzer *Green Table*, 1992
7 Robert Irwin *Two Running Violet V Forms*, 1983
8 Elizabeth Murray *Red Shoe*, 1996
9 Bruce Nauman *Vices and Virtues*, 1988
10 Nam June Paik *Something Pacific*, 1986
11 Niki de Saint Phalle *Sun God*, 1983
12 Alexis Smith *Snake Path*, 1992
13 Kiki Smith *Standing*, 1998
14 William Wegman *La Jolla Vista View*, 1988

Short video programs about each work are available for viewing at the Playback Center in the Undergraduate Library.

Guided tours for large groups can be arranged by advanced request by calling 858/534-2117.

Metered parking is available throughout the campus, or visitors may purchase parking permits at information kiosks or the campus Parking Office. Parking is free on weekends.

The Stuart Collection UCSD
9500 Gilman Drive Dept 0010
La Jolla California 92093-0010
phone 858/534-2117
fax 858/534-9713
web stuartcollection.ucsd.edu

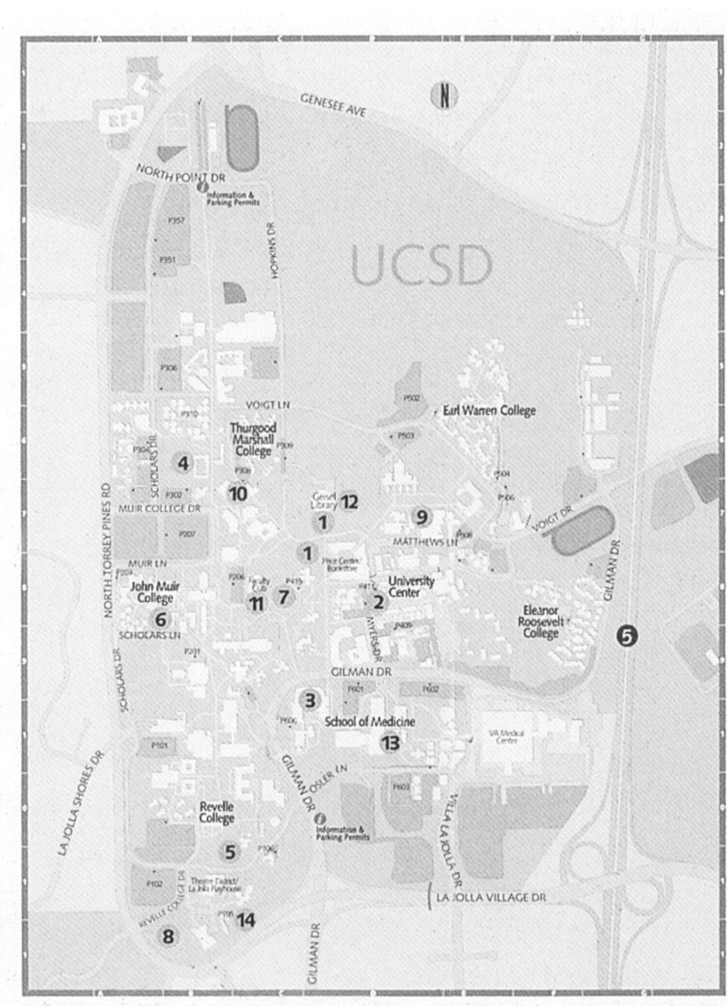

181

180
Snake Path, 'scales' of snake, paving detail

181
Snake Path, UCSD Stuart Collection, plan

182
Snake Path, Central Library plaza, head of snake

183
Snake Path, coiled tail of snake

182

183

ANDREW SPURLOCK MARTIN POIRIER | 917 NINTH AVENUE | SAN DIEGO, CA 92101
T 619 233 3324 | F 619 233 6256

SPURLOCK POIRIER is a regional landscape architectural practice based in Southern California. Many of their projects are expressions of the interaction of a like-minded group of architects, landscape architects and builders. The prevailing design idiom is both purely functional and fully imaginative at once.

ANDREW SPURLOCK established the firm in 1988 to provide an innovative, site-conditioned approach to both planning and landscape architectural design. Martin Poirier joined Spurlock in 1988. The partners had worked together in previous associations going back to 1981. Spurlock Poirier projects include fine-textured, urban 'infill' housing as well as collaborations with artists on practical realization of conceptual plans. The firm worked with the artist Robert Irwin on the garden at Richard Meier's controversial Getty Center in Los Angeles. They have recently expanded their practice internationally, with several major projects in Japan and Mexico.

Both principals maintain a strong interest and involvement in landscape architectural education and community service. Both Spurlock and Poirier lecture extensively and have served on major San Diego design committees and boards.

SELECTED PROJECTS

Balboa Park Activity Center
San Diego, CA, built 1999

Park View Terrace Family Housing
Poway, CA, built 1999

Oak Crest Park
Chula Vista, CA, built 1999

Aztec Walk Master Plan
San Diego State University, San Diego, CA, design 1999

Camino Del Mar Streetscape Plan
Camino Del Mar, CA, design 1998

City Links Vision for City of San Diego
San Diego, CA, design 1997

University of California, San Diego North Campus Master Plan
La Jolla, CA, design 1994

Culver City Downtown Streetscape Improvement Plan
Culver City, CA, built 1992

San Dieguito River Valley Concept Plan
San Diego County, CA, design 1991

J Street Inn/Island Inn Single Room Occupancy Hotels
San Diego, CA, built 1990

SELECTED BIBLIOGRAPHY

ALBERT WARSON AND GAVIN KEENEY, "Stadium Parade Goes on With Montreal, San Diego Designs"
Architectural Record (June 2000)

STEVE CANTOR, "Innovative Design Solutions in Landscape Architecture"
(New York: Van Nostrand Reinhold, 1997)

ROMA DESIGN GROUP – SAN FRANCISCO

MYTHOS, PATHOS AND ETHOS

On October 17, 1989 at 5:04 p.m. the San Francisco Bay Region was rocked by a 7.1 magnitude earthquake centered in the Loma Prieta area of the Santa Cruz mountains 60 miles south-south-east of the City. A 5.2 magnitude aftershock struck 37 minutes after the main event and a tsunami crashed into Monterey Bay, south of San Francisco. The result was widespread structural, ecological and psychic damage. Californians notoriously live in a state of grace – in between natural disasters – or in what cultural historian and critic Mike Davis has recently characterized as the "ecology of fear". This psychological landscape has only recently, however, significantly altered the way West Coast city planners do business. Stringent building codes have been in place for decades, but until the 1989 quake urban infrastructure was simply rebuilt or reinforced after the occasional irruption of cyclic calamities of one kind or another. Mud slides, wildfires, riots and earthquakes all tend to be quickly re-sublimated in architectural terms, in California, which leads in turn to the reliving of the same disasters over and over again.

After the 1989 quake, however, something else happened. CalTrans – the state department of transportation – determined that the damaged Embarcadero Freeway could be reinforced and left in place despite heavy damage from the surface wave of the quake. The San Francisco-Oakland Bridge – the elevated span moved 5 in. to the north – was clearly destined to be patched and reopened but the Embarcadero Freeway was ceremoniously dismantled – after much debate – liberating vast areas of the waterside for new at-grade, tree-lined avenues, parks and generally a liberal outlay of non-commercial public open space. This accidental destruction of the highway essentially sponsored a massive redesign of approaches to the harbor as well as the main commuter

184
Suisun Town Plaza,
Suisun City, CA,
plaza and docks

185
Suisun Town Plaza,
gardens and gazebo

186
Suisun Town Plaza,
plaza,
canal, slips

184

185|186

ferry terminal at the foot of Market Street. ROMA Design Group was selected for the redesign of the Ferry Terminal and the Mid-Embarcadero streetscape based on their 30-year history of designing public open space with a focus on pedestrian culture. The plan stitches together the high-rise downtown financial district and the recreational, commercial, transport facilities of the Embarcadero piers.

ROMA is an urban planning, architectural and landscape architectural services bureau embodying somewhat contradictory impulses. Often associated with the new urbanist movement, ROMA is actually outside the mere reactionary element of that 1980s urban planning idiom and more closely allied with the non-ideological design of contemporary public open space. New Urbanism's implicit elitism is completely lacking in ROMA projects. The scope and detail of the projects ROMA undertakes is a reflection of a concern for urban landscape that transcends financial and social programming, the ghost in the machine underwriting most New Urbanist projects. Suisun City Town Plaza (c. 1995) is an integrated redevelopment of the waterside facilities – marina, train station, and live-work fabric – central to the identity of the city.

ROMA combines ecological, landscape-architectural and public infrastructural concerns to produce conditions conducive to fostering social and cultural interaction versus picturesque, socially irresponsible and elitist urban and suburban enclaves. The texture and ambiance of ROMA projects picture a sensibility of 'open' urbanism, eschewing the hegemony of the superblock and the concomitant tangle of overlapping infrastructural systems re-envisioned in current architectural practice as simply "extra-large" forms of single-volume architecture. ROMA's recent urban design work follows on the 1970s and 1980s wave of exploitative commercial infill in desperate urban areas – post-industrial waterfronts and benighted inner-city neighborhoods – but employs a greater flexibility and more generous spirit in doling out uncontaminated public open space.

187

188

MID-EMBARCADERO — SAN FRANCISCO

The Mid-Embarcadero area benefited immensely from the 1989 earthquake. After the demolition of the elevated roadway links to the financial district were restored through links to Justin Herman Plaza and the public byways wending through the office towers crowding the city grid north of Market Street.

The tree-lined avenue is scaled to permit a generous pedestrian concourse and 'voluble' groves of trees. The plan centers on the clock tower of the Ferry Terminal, which is on axis with Market Street. Paving details and street furnishings direct pedestrian traffic to the entrance to the ferry slips and the facade of the terminal building establishes the breadth of the public square.

Cable cars travel the central median separating the dual roadway and multiple transport systems nearby supply options for commuters entering and leaving the downtown. The BART (Bay Area Rapid Transit) Embarcadero subway station on Market Street is the main route out of the downtown (it runs below Market Street) and various bus lines connect to the Transbay Transit Terminal further up Market Street.

187
Mid-Embarcadero,
San Francisco, CA,
aerial view of ferry terminal,
freeway and
Justin Herman Plaza
before earthquake

188
Mid-Embarcadero,
music concourse

189

190

191

192

189
*Mid-Embarcadero,
aerial view of
financial district*

190
*Mid-Embarcadero,
ferry terminal
and San Francisco Bay
(after demolition of freeway)*

191 | 192
*Mid-Embarcadero,
bird's-eye views of proposed
ferry terminal*

193

194

195

193
Mid-Embarcadero,
Pier 7,
tall ships

194
Downtown Ferry
Terminal,
San Francisco, CA,
sketch of bird's-eye view of
proposed new slips

195
Downtown Ferry
Terminal,
sketch of view from water
approaching terminal

DOWNTOWN FERRY TERMINAL — SAN FRANCISCO

ROMA's Downtown Ferry Terminal is another piece in the ongoing resurrection of San Francisco's historic waterfront. Following the conversion of several piers to public and tourist facilities, the centrally located Ferry Terminal has long been touted as the gateway to Marin and the north counties. The renovated building and piers will integrate new federally-mandated intermodal transportation systems – water, rail, walking, cycling and road systems – while creating a pedestrian promenade showcasing the historic warehouse and pier architecture of the waterfront which receives hordes of tourists a year. The 1896 Ferry Building, which is not quake-proof, is also to be redesigned to higher standards of seismic resistance and opened to additional public functions. ROMA's role as urban planners has been to integrate these various programmatic elements while ensuring a surplus of user-driven open space.

A legendary, perhaps ferocious 'ley' line crosses the floor of San Francisco Bay and penetrates into the heart of the financial district, the high-rise heart of downtown. Perhaps lined with veins of gold and silver, this energetic current can be sensed while crossing the bay on one of the many ferries connecting the affluent, northerly communities of Tiburon, Sausalito, Larkspur and Vallejo to downtown San Francisco.

The redesigned ferry terminal will feature new amenities and waiting areas for passengers – both queuing and disembarking – and new slips and berths for hovercraft. As the main commuter gateway to the City, the terminal handles thousands of people a day. The tourist ferries to the northwest – leaving Fishermans Wharf for Sausalito, Tiburon and Alcatraz – are intentionally separated from this main portal due to the overwhelming number of day visitors drawn to the Embarcadero restaurants and amusements.

196

196
U.S. Courthouse, Sacramento
CA, Sacramento,
Redevelopment Area,
Union Pacific Railyards
(left center)

U.S. COURTHOUSE AND FEDERAL BUILDING — SACRAMENTO

ROMA's contribution to the U.S. Courthouse and Federal Building in the state capitol is part of a larger urban planning scheme for the Union Pacific railyards, a 175-acre brownfield north of downtown Sacramento.

The Courthouse serves the typical role of providing an impression of grandeur while acting as a gateway to the railyards redevelopment nearby. The entry plaza and interiors include public art elements, a 1-percent of budget stipulation of Government Services Administration projects nationwide. The exterior art elements include a waterwall by ROMA and peculiar bronze statuary by artist Tom Otterness of a cartoon-like mode and scale drawing on the historic and mythic character of the Old West. Inscribed pavers by Jenny Holzer will carry legalese *bon mots*.

The practice's role as urban designers includes the study of building massing and the production of plazas and streetscapes. The formal boulevards and courtyards are lavishly planted corridors and passages within a proposed high-density commercial-retail city center. The former infrastructure is integrated into the urban fabric by extending the city grid into the barren railyard and vigorously supplying figural content to the site through modulation of blocks and byways with open space and parks. Modest towers punctuate this new urban field providing orientation and capitalizing on existing transportation systems. The 40-year plan envisions an entirely new city within the city in an area casually but brutally disfigured over the past century. 37 acres of toxic cleanup has already been carried out. The new residential quarter along the river reserves the choicest parcels for the full re-colonization of an industrial and post-industrial wasteland.

197

198

199

197
U.S. Courthouse Plaza,
bench and water wall

198
U.S. Courthouse Plaza,
entry piers

199
U.S. Courthouse Plaza,
plaza and steps
(with Otterness wagon train)

ROMA DESIGN GROUP | 1527 STOCKTON STREET | SAN FRANCISCO, CA 94133
T 415 616 9900 | F 415 788 8728

ROMA DESIGN GROUP is a nationally recognized urban design and planning firm with over 30 years of experience in a variety of projects affecting the growth and development of American communities. Projects include both public and private commissions in urban and suburban settings focused primarily on the West Coast of the United States.

ROMA also undertakes selected projects abroad, including most recently the Coal Harbour mixed-use development in Vancouver, British Columbia; the downtown plan for Manila; a mixed-use complex in downtown Kuala Lumpur; and an architectural study of an American consulate in Santo Domingo.

ROMA specializes in revitalization of urban infill sites, typified by their well-known Third Street Promenade in Santa Monica, CA and the recent renovation of the Mid-Embarcadero in San Francisco, CA. These projects exemplify the ongoing nature of modern urban design, a paradigm that is essentially based on constant change. The urban design projects all are inherently public projects, albeit with a mixed source of funding, with commercial components strategically located as a means of fostering critical mass.

SELECTED PROJECTS

Mid-Embarcadero
San Francisco, CA, built 2000

Playa Vista Community Plan
Los Angeles, CA, design 1999

1221 Ocean Avenue
Santa Monica, CA, built 1999

Downtown Ferry Terminal
San Francisco, CA, design c. 1999

U.S. Courthouse and Federal Building
Sacramento, CA, built 1999

Suisun City Town Plaza
Suisun City, CA, built c. 1995

Downtown Plan and Streetscape Design
Santa Cruz, CA, design c. 1991

Orchard Road Concept Development
Singapore, design c. 1999

Third Street Promenade
Santa Monica, CA, built 1990

Pier 7, Mid-Embarcadero
San Francisco, CA, built c. 1985

SELECTED BIBLIOGRAPHY

ARNOLD BERKE, "Turnaround Town"
Historic Preservation (March 1996)

AARON BETSKY, "The City by the Bay Goes from Port to Sport"
[Embarcadero], Architectural Record (March 1996)

BORIS DRAMOV, "Successful Waterfront Design Principles"
Urban Land (June 1997)

BORIS DRAMOV, BONNIE FISHER, "Downtown Ferry Terminal San Francisco"
Aquapolis (March 1997)

BONNIE FISHER, "From the Water's Edge"
Urban Land (January 1999)

BONNIE FISHER, "Successful Base Redevelopments"
Urban Land (July 1996)

DIANA KETCHUM, "Suisun City: New Life for a Lost Community"
Architectural Record (June 1995)

CHARLES LOCKWOOD, "On the Waterfront: San Francisco Embarcadero Waterfront"
World Architecture (July-August 1997)

CHARLES LOCKWOOD, "Pioneering Petaluma"
Planning (October 1998)

CHARLES LOCKWOOD, "San Francisco Reclaims its Downtown Waterfront"
Urban Land (October 1996)

CHARLES LOCKWOOD, "Suisun City, California"
Urban Land (May 1995)

CHARLES LOCKWOOD, "Urban Oases"
Hemispheres (September 1996)

KEVIN POWELL, "Finding Common Ground"
[Third Street Promenade, Santa Monica, CA], Landscape Architecture (July 1992)

J. WILLIAM THOMPSON, "Embarcadero: Free from the Freeway"
Landscape Architecture (June 1993)

"Millennial Face-Lift"
[Embarcadero], Landscape Architecture (May 1998)

CIVITAS AND GRAVITAS

Achva Stein's work in Los Angeles and Israel involves the intense cultivation of natural and cultural resources, simultaneously. Her urban projects for Los Angeles are community-based efforts intended to breathe new life into areas either abandoned or under-utilized. Stein's urban parks and gardens are the antithesis of the passive green spaces of traditional American urban parks. They are derived from an Old World ethic that considers the cultivation of land a virtue and a New World ethic that embraces a large measure of chaos and indecidability in urban planning.

This land ethic is partly a product of Achva Stein's experience of Israeli kibbutzim, where intensive collaborative agricultural efforts are the foundation of community life. Stein's Hula Valley project (c. 1986), between the Galilean and Golan Heights – the latter where the headwaters of the Jordan River rise – is a comprehensive plan to acknowledge the necessary interdependence of industrial production, nature reserves, and agriculture.

The Hula Valley is a diverse wetland environment and serves, today, as a recreational zone for tourists as well as the local Jewish-Arabic population. Systematically drained and converted to agricultural lands in the mid-20th century, modern exigencies have focused attention on environmental management and restoration efforts – plus mitigation of the increased accommodation of guests to the valley. The area is host to thousands of migratory birds, and a nature reserve – established in 1961 – protects vital marsh and papyrus beds associated with an extinct prehistoric lake. The precious nature of water in the Mid-East makes this area an important and strategic component in the regional aquifer. Ongoing plans include reforestation of denuded tracts vital to stabilizing soil and managing water resources; recreational activities utilizing existing canals, reservoirs and trail systems; and modest (light) agricultural activities in the form of grazing, bee-keeping and light forestry. Local kibbutzim – extant farm communities – would benefit from increased economic activity by hosting tourists and managing the forest and agricultural reserves.

200
Hula Valley, Israel, aerial view of contested area

201
Hula Valley, Recreational, Forestry and Conservation Plans

200

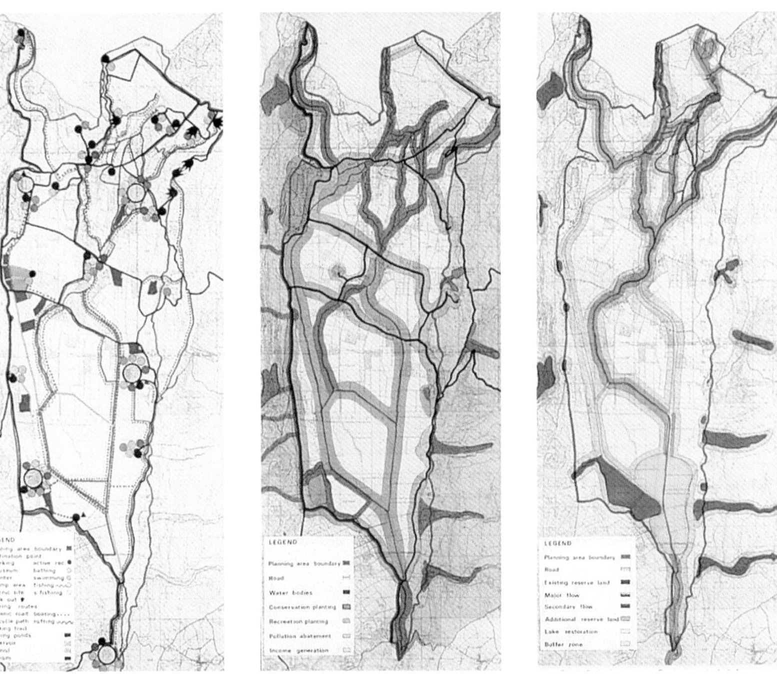
LEGEND
Planning area boundary
Destination point
parking
active rec
museum
bathing
center
swimming
camp area
fishing
picnic site
s. fishing
Look out
Touring routes
scenic road
boating
bicycle path
rafting
hiking trail
Fishing ponds
Reservoir
Stream
LEGEND
Planning area boundary
Road
Water bodies
Conservation planting
Recreation planting
Pollution abatement
Income generation
LEGEND
Planning area boundary
Road
Existing reserve land
Major flow
Secondary flow
Additional reserve land
Lake restoration
Buffer zone

201

202

203

Another project in the region, the restoration plan for the Faradis Quarry (c. 1985), is a dialectical exercise mediating conflicting claims of Arab and Jewish settlements through creation of a garden that adopts both Islamic and Jewish motifs. The Roman-era limestone quarry is located at the southern end of the Carmel Mountain range, midway between Haifa and Tel Aviv, in the Zichron Yaakov area. The garden, set in the basin of the quarry, is an orchard with a processional route passing up the middle to a reflecting pool at the base of the rock face. A grove of figs is planted in irrigated channels reminiscent of Moorish, Moghul and Persian courtyard gardens. The central tree-lined promenade is an allusion to Jewish settlement practices of planting windscreens bordering agricultural lands. The chiseled face of the quarry is the symbolic *terra infirma*. The sublime scenic landscape beyond the quarry may be taken from the bluffs above the garden.

The prevailing urban design strategy of the studio, influenced by these planning projects, is to increase activity in benighted parts of the city through creation of gardens and educational activities bringing the local population together through processes of discovery and reclamation of existing landscape resources. Contrary to reactionary efforts to gentrify or aesthetically codify urban open space – usually as a precursor to massive real estate re-investment and the influx of middle and upper class economic activity – the work of Achva Stein is simply and purposely understated. Its role in urban landscape design is more the amelioration of total chaos than the wholesale redesign of urban décor called for by public planners.

202
Hula Valley, forestry

203
Hula Valley, drainage ditch

204
Faradis Quarry, Zichron Yaakov, Israel, axonometric of proposal

205
Faradis Quarry, view of site

206
Faradis Quarry, sketch of cypress allée

207
Faradis Quarry, sketch of precipice and ficus grove

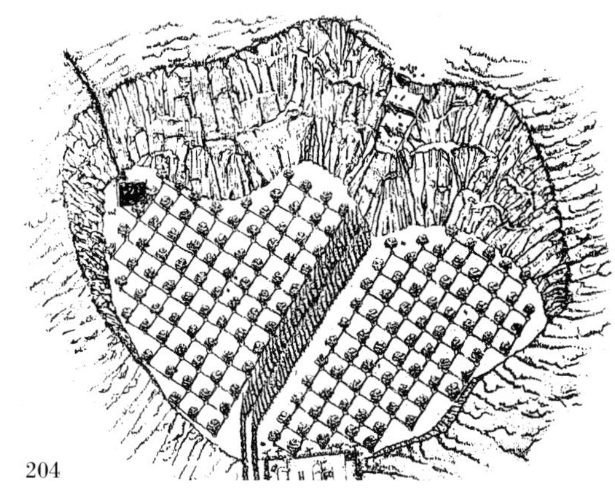

204

205

206

207

208

CARMELITOS GARDEN — LOS ANGELES

Urban projects like Carmelitos Garden and Uhuru Garden are conscious efforts to revitalize communities essentially marginalized in the Los Angeles metropolitan area. The highly structured urban parks match the tight-knit nature of the communities they serve and are meant as socially progressive venues countering the anonymity of corporate and institutional American urban pseudo-public space.

Carmelito's racial makeup, a housing development dating to 1941, is 17 percent Hispanic, 25 percent White, 55 percent African-American and 3 percent other – the latter a statistical 'double Other'. It is a low-rent district with approximately 8 000 residents. The proposed gardens would function as a training center for greenhouse management, landscape gardening, irrigation installation and maintenance, and tree care. It would also incorporate a farmers market and an amphitheater, becoming in part a commercial venture. Vegetable, herb and fruit garden plots would be tended by residents.

208
Carmelitos Garden, Carmelitos, CA, isometric

209
Carmelitos Garden, vegetable gardens

210
Carmelitos Garden, children's section

209

210

211

UHURU GARDEN — LOS ANGELES

The 2-acre garden is a collage of services and amenities implanted into a neighborhood renowned for its anarchic mix of subcultures. Both culturally and horticulturally ambitious, the garden is an urban refuge or oasis. The block is laced with temporal usage that gives it a mutable, vital souk-like atmosphere consistent with Frederick Turner's "nonlinear tragicomic model" for post-cultural landscape described in the essay *Landscape of Disturbance* as transitional zones undergoing continuous change and nourished by ecologically inspired ideas of social and human economy.

The Watts neighborhood is at best ragtag and the open spaces of the housing projects are lethal, inhuman surveillance zones. Achva Stein applied sustainable concepts to the human ecology of the Los Angeles inner city quarter through multiple overlapping programs aimed at enlivening the links between interstitial landscape, residential complexes and civic institutions.

A work and recreation space, the garden is an open-air marketplace organized around plots devoted to utilitarian and aesthetic activities. The garden provides historic perspective on traditional land use in Southern California through representational landscape forms and, at the same time, work opportunities and agricultural production (the latter to be sold, *in situ*, at the farmers market). The overall structure and the interior subdivision of landscape types convey a concern for complexity and a modicum of respect for formal order. As bazaar, the garden is a rich mosaic of forces 'held in tension' through the unifying vision of an island of civility amid the turmoil of inner city Los Angeles.

211
Uhuru Garden, Watts, Los Angeles, CA, bird's-eye view of proposal

212
Uhuru Garden, aspects of energy education

213
Uhuru Garden, examples of typical Californian natural environments

214
Uhuru Garden, elements of Californian cultural landscape

215
Uhuru Garden, plan / montage

212 | 213

214 | 215

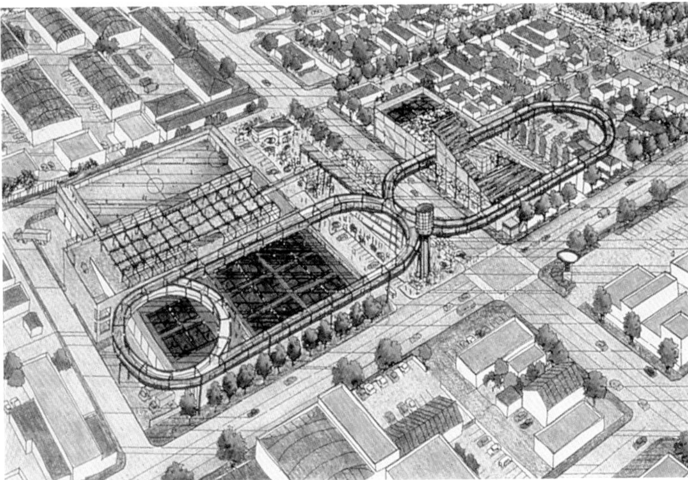

216

LA BREA GATEWAY AND 10 MINIPARKS – WEST HOLLYWOOD/LOS ANGELES

La Brea Gateway is part of the redevelopment program for down-at-the-heels West Hollywood, where east-west Santa Monica Boulevard intersects north-south La Brea Avenue in a region noted more for its proximity to the Hollywood Bowl, Griffith Park, and Hollywood Boulevard, all north of Sunset Boulevard, than for any intrinsic identity of its own. The CRA plan – Commercial Recreation Area Plan – is both an averaging of the usual urban revitalization schemes and a subtle critique of the type. The planned racetrack-like elevated platform, formally an amusement zone, is also a circuit linking the figurative divide between north and south Los Angeles, a divide that is marked in fact – in actuality – not by Santa Monica Boulevard but by Wilshire Boulevard. This social geography is reinforced by the automobile culture that rules Los Angeles. Classes rarely mix in Los Angeles as a result of this existing north-south stratification.

As the low-rise texture of Los Angeles rarely affords views of the City or of the surrounding landscape, the layered plan offers rooftop escapades in the form of sports facilities and pedestrian promenades. The observation tower mimics the observatory at Griffith Park (located in a park high above the City), allowing Angelinos to view the sprawling metropolis instead from within.
In the ramp-escalator-and-elevator-serviced areas of the sides and tops of the buildings the subject of urban spectacle is addressed, as is urban gentrification in the Lexington Avenue street plan. The texture of the housing district is carefully calibrated to avoid the picturesque blandness of the thoroughfares, signifying a district axially opposed to the avenues. Accommodation of parking is

216
La Brea Gateway, West Hollywood, CA, bird's-eye view of proposal

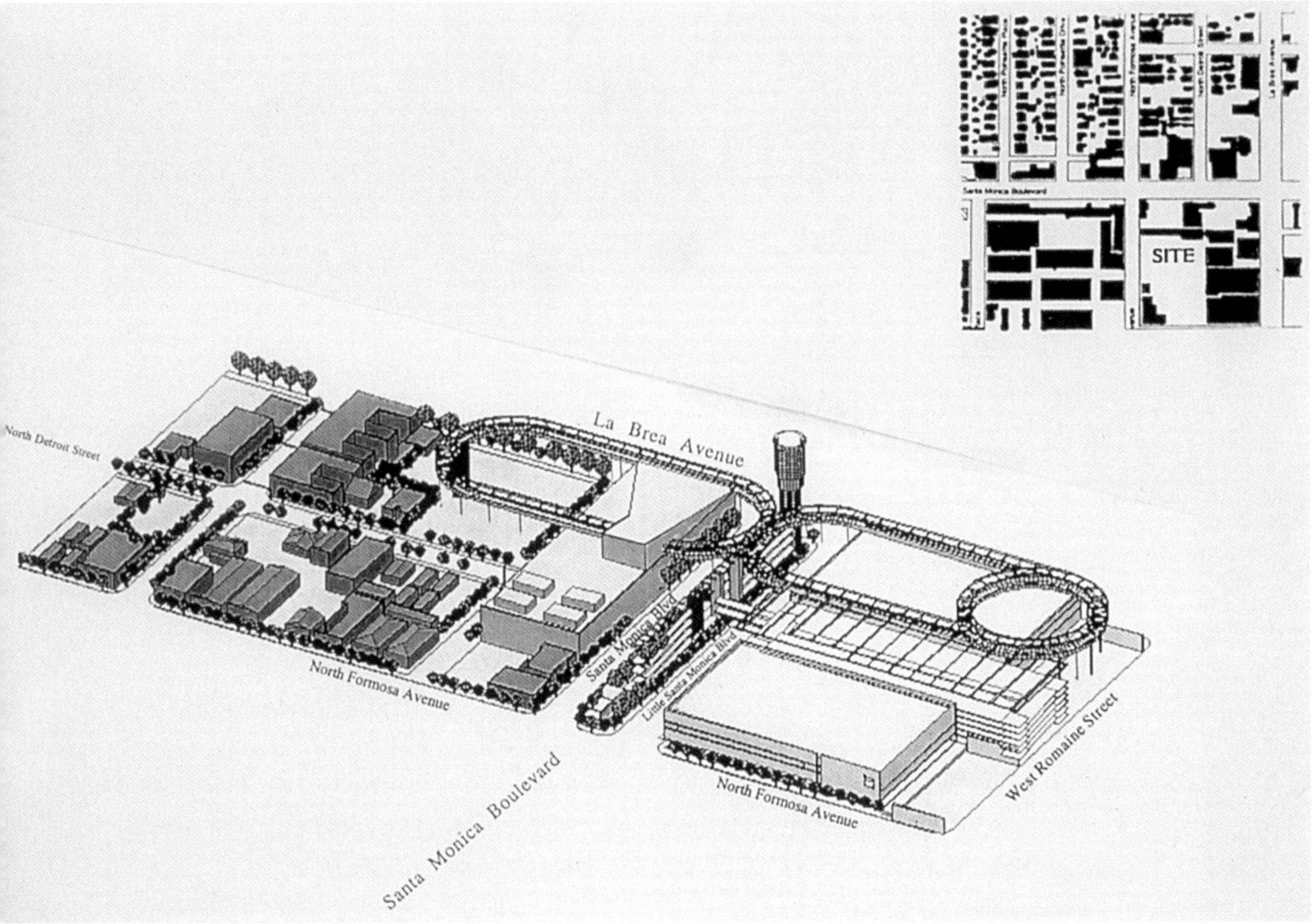

217

218

219

217
La Brea Gateway, axonometric of proposal

218
La Brea Gateway, perspective of ramps and bridges

219
La Brea Gateway, perspective of observation tower

220 | 221

222 | 223

built into the refurbished blocks and big-box retail is programmed to anchor the commercial aspect of the project. These elements are predictable and the necessary means of funding for this public-private partnership. Stein's proposal seems to incorporate all the conventional gestures of contemporary urbanism while undermining those typologies from within by acknowledging Los Angeles's essentially exuberant heterogeneous culture – often a culture of excess most cogently expressed in the amusement park at Santa Monica Pier, at the western end of the Boulevard.

The human dimension of urban and landscape planning is the focus of other complex, but mostly low-tech projects. Modest in nature, their cumulative effect is transformational. Stein's 10 Miniparks project for South-Central Los Angeles – commissioned by the Community Redevelopment Agency following the April 1992 riots – studied the visual and social implications of the looted and burned sections of the city. The riots were in part contained by the Los Angeles police force by letting the enraged African-American community effectively destroy their own neighborhoods. The intention of the sketch studies was to suggest a series of parks, gardens and markets that might raise the quality of life while major redevelopment projects for housing, commerce, and infrastructure were under review. The before-after sketches illustrate the modest resources required to alter considerably the everyday experience of life in the streets of South-Central Los Angeles.

220 | 221 | 222 | 223
Miniparks,
Los Angeles, CA,
before-after sketches
of two examples

ACHVA BENZINBERG STEIN & ASSOCIATES | 1116 DIAMOND AVENUE
SOUTH PASADENA, CA 91030
T 626 441 3693 | F 626 441 4984

ACHVA BENZINBERG STEIN, a graduate of Harvard University and the University of California, Berkeley, is Chair of the department of Landscape Architecture at North Carolina State University. Previously she was Director and Associate Professor of the Landscape Architecture Program at the University of Southern California, Los Angeles. Stein is a practicing professional who has taught, lectured and worked in the US, Europe, Israel, India and China. From 1981–1986, Stein practiced in Haifa, Israel on government housing and conservation plans.
She has received numerous grants for urban design projects, including support from the National Endowment for the Arts for the Uhuru Garden in Watts. In her practice she concentrates on work which involves participatory planning with neighborhood groups, public housing agencies and non-profit organizations. Achva Benzinberg Stein & Associates was established in 1994. Recent projects include designs for housing, school grounds, parks, playgrounds, and private residences. Stein has received numerous awards for her community-based service. These include Chrysler Award for Innovation in Design, Certificate of Commendation for Outstanding Service to the Community from the City of Los Angeles, Council of Educators in Landscape Architecture Award of Distinction, USC Associates Awards for Excellence in Teaching, and Association of Collegiate Schools of Architecture Collaborative Practice Award. Stein's book *Moroccan Gardens and Courtyards* – a photographic essay - is forthcoming from Thames and Hudson.

SELECTED PROJECTS

Multnoma Schoolyard
(w/ North East Trees), Los Angeles, CA, built 2000

Carmelitos
Los Angeles, CA, built 1999

Richardson Park
Los Angeles, CA, built 1999

Uyemura Residence
Newport Beach, CA, built 1998

Blessed Rock Senior Citizen Housing
El Monte, CA, built 1998

Non-Motorized Plan for Southern California
(w/ Futterman and Associates), Los Angeles, CA, design 1997

La Brea Gateway
West Hollywood, CA, design 1995

Uhuru Garden
(w/ BLS Environmental Planning and Design), Los Angeles, CA, design 1993

10 Miniparks
(w/ Bernstein and Stein), Los Angeles, CA, design c. 1992

Conservation Plan for the Jordan River and Hula Valley
(Achva Benzinberg Stein, Landscape Architect), Israel, design (partial implementation) c. 1986

Faradis Quarry
(Achva Benzinberg Stein, Landscape Architect), Israel Ministry of Agriculture, Israel, design 1985

SELECTED BIBLIOGRAPHY

AARON BETSKY, "Uhuru Garden, Watts, Los Angeles"
Landscape Architecture (December 1992)

GUY COOPER AND GORDON TAYLOR, Paradise Transformed: The Private Garden for the 21st Century
(New York: Monacelli Press, 1996)

RUSSELL FERGUSON (ED.), Urban Revisions: Current Projects for the Public Realm
(Los Angeles: MOCA, 1994)

MARK FRANCIS AND RANDOLF T. HESTER, The Meaning of Gardens: Idea, Place and Action
(Cambridge: MIT Press, 1991)

DIANE GHIRARDO, "Architecture in Los Angeles"
Arquitectura Viva (December 1991)

MORRIS NEWMAN, "Los Angeles' Defensible Parks"
Landscape Architecture (February 1995)

JAMES GRAYSON TRULOVE, The New American Garden: Innovations in Residential Landscape Architecture
(New York: Whitney Library of Design, 1998)

ACHVA STEIN, JACQUELINE CLAIRE MOXLEY, "In Defense of the Non Natives"
[The Case of the Eucalyptus], Landscape Journal (Spring 1992)

ACHVA STEIN, "Topic Studio: Nature, Landscape and Garden"
Journal of Architectural Education (April 1991)

ACHVA STEIN, NORMAN MILLAR, "Windows of Opportunity: Reprogramming Residual Urban Space"
Landscape Journal (Special Issue 1998)

"Eco-Revelatory Design: Nature Constructed/Nature Revealed"
[Exhibition reviews by Brenda Brown, Richard Haag, Robert L. Thayer], Landscape Journal, (Special Issue 1998)

INFRASTRUCTURE AND ANXIETY

The work of GLS – Gary Leonard Strang – explores the relationship of urban infrastructure to urban open space and architectural landscape in a complex mode between site planning and detailed installation work. Strang's premise that infrastructure should be revealed versus concealed is inspired in part by Lewis Mumford's critique of the City Beautiful Movement of the late-19th and early-20th centuries. This classicist vision engendered schemes for the picturesque re-making of American cities requiring the burial and concealment of all signs of industrial production and modern technical services. A Romantic Classical model, the 'lofty idealism' of the City Beautiful movement was an alternative to Tony Garnier's *Cité Industrielle* (1917) and Sant'Elia's *Città Nuova* (1914), where an industrial picturesque was proposed by clearly valorizing and integrating the rational architectural language of industrial production. The latter models mostly prevailed and were the precursors to Constructivist, Functionalist and Bauhaus architectural production.

GLS has primarily sought to unearth hidden resources within the city. These underground systems include hydrological, utility and conveyance systems typically designed to vanish below the aestheticized surface of streets, plazas and parks. This fascination with sub-grade and above-grade infrastructure was a product of his years working on infill housing projects with architect Dan Solomon in San Francisco. Such projects revealed the ubiquity and *ad hoc* engineering rationale of modern utilities. The studio personally constructs many of their projects and as a result manages to find unforeseen opportunities in the process for enhancing the problematic of the design.

Steam Temple (1994) with Michael Roche utilized the site of an abandoned WPA-era public bath on the Lower East Side of Manhattan to create a steam sculpture/temple. The study was funded by the Public Art Fund and exhibited at the Paine Webber Gallery in Manhattan. The Public Art Fund proposed that Strang work with Con Edison – the New York utility – to select a site for the hypothetical temple. Consistent with the conventional wisdom that steam wafting from the streets of New York connotes a 'break' or a 'rupture' in the underground lines, Con Edison declined to participate. Undeterred, Strang's temple celebrated both the existing underground steam tunnels that produce plumes of steam in winter on New York streets – not indicative of any specific

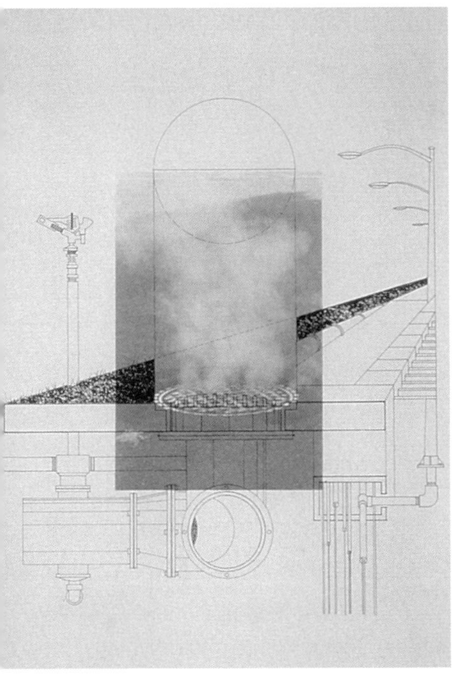

224

225

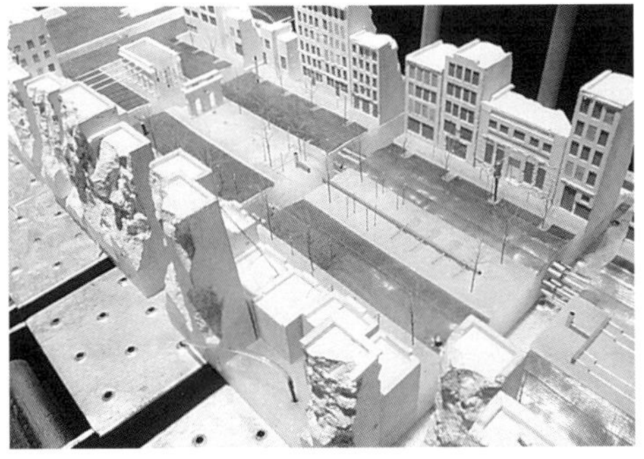

226

227

224
Steam Temple,
New York City, NY,
exposed structure,
montage

225
Steam Temple,
street with steam vents

226|227
Steam Temple,
model

228

229

230

underground problems – and the hypothetical tapping of geological substrata, an idea now taken quite seriously with the advent of thermal pumps. More appropriate to Iceland than New York City – on a purely practical level – tapping underground energy systems is nonetheless an apt metaphor for accessing unrealized potential below the tarmac.

Herman Park Water Basin proposed creating a basin to collect seasonal floodwater within a Houston park designed by George Kessler, a *protégé* of Frederick Law Olmsted. Prepared for a design competition, the plan for the basin included the planting of bald cypress trees, a species that inhabits the bayous of coastal Texas and Louisiana. Rather than evacuating the seasonal rains, the proposal would store the water in an earth-banked basin as an *impromptu* reflecting pool reminiscent of the pool in Washington, D.C. between the Lincoln Memorial and the Washington Monument. The existing obelisk would be temporarily 'cast adrift'. The waters would however slowly evaporate (in the summer) revealing underlying gardens and a more modest pool. Overflow would be directed into an adjacent lake.

These strategies are consistent with themes explored in Anne Whiston Spirn's *The Granite Garden: Urban Nature and Human Design* (1984). Revealing the cyclic rhythms of nature in the city has become a minor theme – albeit usually a discordant anti-theme – in contemporary urban design. Tying these experiences to the complex web of infrastructure above and below ground is a provocative technique for altering the perceived mutual exclusivity of built and natural systems.

228
Herman Park Water Basin, Houston, TX, aerial view of existing park

229
Herman Park Water Basin, perspective of gardens

230
The Lofts, San Francisco, CA, dumpster and propane tank bollards

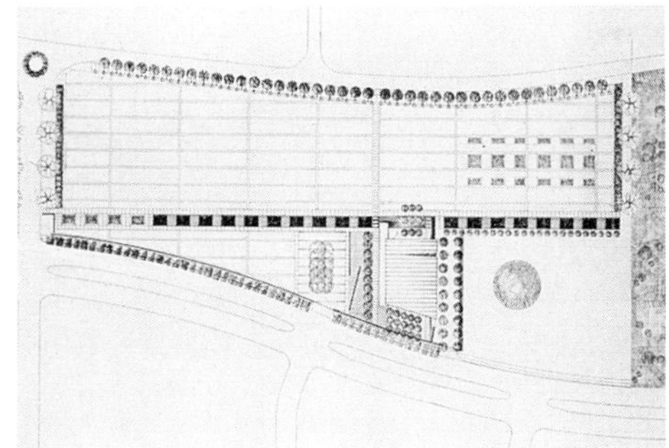

231

232

BETH ISRAEL MEMORIAL GARDEN — HOUSTON WITH DAN SOLOMON ARCHITECT

A collaborative project with architect Dan Solomon, Beth Israel Chapel in Houston, Texas is a small urban memorial garden with a chapel open to the elements and built out of simple, sturdy materials. Its elegant, spare aesthetic is derived from a synthesis of materiality – concrete, steel, aluminum and mahogany details – and ambient environmental elements that 'index' the cyclic rhythms of nature.

The chapel and gardens were added to an existing Jewish cemetery within the larger system of a traditional park-like Christian burial ground. The 3-acre site will eventually contain 19 small mausolea for the interment of ashes, while the majority of burials take place in the green lawn marked by stones flush with the grass surface.

A slit in the roof of the 7000-sq.-ft. chapel illumines the interior – not unlike the Pantheon in Rome – and rainwater collected from the roof streams into an elevated concrete trough that frames the entrance to the garden. Channeled into a seasonal pool in the garden, the rainwater (50–100 in. per year) forms a reflective backdrop for the memorial services. The 10-ft.-by-50-ft. pool overflows into drainage tiles beneath the walkways that cross the garden, disappearing into underground crushed rock basins and, eventually, into the Houston underground storm-water system. A row of birches edging the 600-ft. main avenue through the garden is cabled to opposing canted poles and will form an arbor over time.

231
Beth Israel Memorial Garden, Houston, TX, site plan

232
Beth Israel Memorial Garden, model of chapel

233
Beth Israel Memorial Garden, chapel through trees

158

234

234
Beth Israel Memorial Garden, chapel and fountain pool

235
Beth Israel Memorial Garden, perforated anodized aluminum entry gates

235

238 | 239

236

237

236
Beth Israel Memorial Garden, concrete slabs for future mausolea

237
Beth Israel Memorial Garden, entrance walk

238
Beth Israel Memorial Garden, chapel 'portico'

239
Beth Israel Memorial Garden, detail of chapel and fountain pool

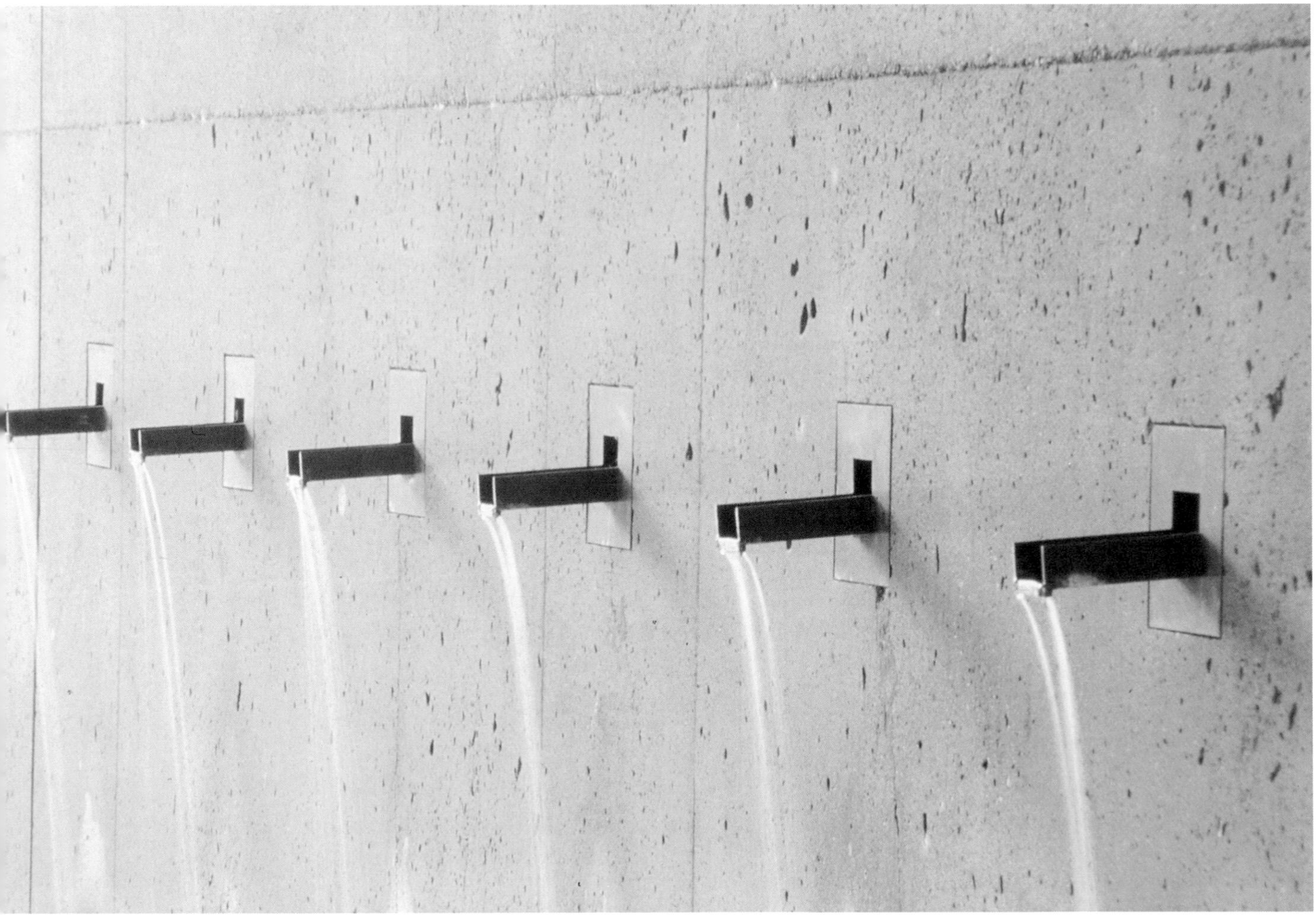

240

241

240
Beth Israel
Memorial Garden,
interior scuppers

241
Beth Israel
Memorial Garden,
memorial wall

THREE EXHIBITIONS

WATER WORKS — FORT MASON WITH MICHAEL ROCHE

Water Works was a 5-day installation for the 1992 Golden Gate Park Fort Mason Pier annual art festival. The project is an intentionally fetishistic, irrigated piece of turf elevated on a canted scaffold. It serves as an exposé or critique of the predictable annual exhibits by landscape contractors at Fort Mason, 95 percent of which are lovely, floriferous gardens reminiscent of those staged each year at the Chelsea Flower Show in London.

The 25 temporary landscapes installed at Fort Mason Pier each took a piece of the well-known Monopoly board game as inspiration – in this case the property chosen was "Utilities". The existing 12-in. water main at Fort Mason Pier was appropriated as a symbol of all-pervasive infrastructure in the modern city and utilized to conceptually support the turf installation. The lush stretch of sod critically encapsulates the artificiality of American suburban lawns and gardens in the arid American West, while the supporting apparatus – scaffold, pressurized main and sprinkler system – reveal the necessary but usually concealed life support systems required for maintaining gardens in California.

WURSTER HALL EXHIBITION — BERKELEY WITH MICHAEL ROCHE

Held at the School of Architecture's Wurster Hall, on the campus of the University of California at Berkeley, the 1991 Wurster exhibition was curated by Chip Sullivan, a professor at the School of Architecture known for his comic-book-inspired architectural expressionism.

Gary Strang and Michael Roche's installation proposed to reveal the guts of the 10-story brutalist building legendary for its exposed structure – through an exploration of piping systems crisscrossing the campus, penetrating buildings and linking up to regional and national networks.

242
Water Works, San Francisco, CA, installation with existing water main

243
Water Works, elevation of proposed installation

244
Water Works, plan of proposed installation

242

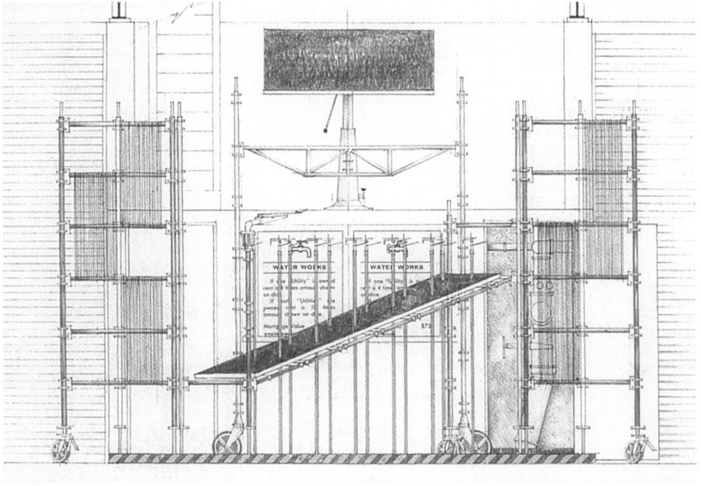

243 | 244

245

The scaffold and the image wall recreate an environment of haphazard infrastructure that inhabits the industrial byways of America underwriting the American Dream of endless prosperity. The scaffold is hung with stretched shade cloth and an image wall plastered with xerox images of piping configurations from various American industrial landscapes. The museological format is intentional and recalls the pseudo-archaeological installations of Mark Dion. Terry Gilliam's renowned film *Brazil* (1985) – with its gurgling, dyspeptic plumbing and ductwork – expressed a similar obsession to Strang's with the 'colonic' dimension of technological society. Strang and Gilliam are both attracted and repulsed by the sinister and dystopian vision of unseen forces irrupting into everyday experience.

EXIT I–80 – SAN FRANCISCO

An exhibition entry for the California College of Arts and Crafts annual lecture series ("Utility and Vicinity" in 1993), the Exit I–80 Embarcadero Freeway ramp was initially saved from demolition, following the 1989 earthquake, but later removed. Reconfigured as a tree-lined blind promenade – going nowhere – in the GLS proposal, the ramp became a vegetated ruin and pedestrian verge for viewing the surrounding spectacle of the Embarcadero streetscape. Trees – with a flexible and fine-textured tracery – are cabled and pulled over the roadbed, in time, to create a tunnel and canopy framing the view to the Bay Bridge.

245
Wurster Hall Exhibition, Berkeley, CA, installation

246
Exit I–80, San Francisco, CA, abandoned ramp with bystanders

247|248
Exit I–80, model views of proposed ramp

247

248

246

GARY L. STRANG | 246 FIRST STREET #306 | SAN FRANCISCO, CA 94105
T 415 227 4084 | F 415 227 4234
gls@slip.net

GARY L. STRANG is an architecture and landscape architecture office established in 1993. Gary Strang is a registered architect and has a Master of Landscape Architecture degree from the University of California at Berkeley. Prior to opening his own office, Gary Strang worked for California architect Dan Solomon. These dual degrees permit Strang to pursue the integration of building and site, a condition central to contemporary design practice. The often mutually exclusive systems and fields are the source for both polemical installation projects and dynamic site-specific projects. GARY STRANG has lectured and taught widely. The office participates in a variety of exhibitions and conferences as a means of exploring the intellectual currents informing contemporary landscape and architectural practice.

SELECTED PROJECTS

Beth Israel Memorial Garden
(w/ Dan Solomon), Houston, TX, built 1996

The Lofts
San Francisco, CA, built 1994

Steam Temple
(Public Art Fund – Urban Paradise: Gardens in the City),
New York City, NY, exhibition 1994

Exit I–80, California College of Arts and Crafts
San Francisco, CA, exhibition 1993

Water Works
(w/ Michael Roche), San Francisco Landscape Garden Show (Golden Gate Park),
San Francisco, CA, exhibition 1992

Herman Park Water Basin
Houston, TX, competition 1992

Infrastructure as Landscape, University of California
Berkeley, CA, exhibition 1991

Manhattan Megadeck - Westside Highway
(Municipal Art Society), New York City, NY, competition 1987

SELECTED BIBLIOGRAPHY

JOSEPH GIOVANNINI, "Sacred Ground"
[Beth Israel Chapel], Architecture (June 1998)

MICHAEL LECCESE, "Improbable Proving Ground"
[University Avenue, Berkeley], Landscape Architecture (February 1997)

MATTHEW POTTEIGER AND JAMIE PURINTON, "Revealing Infrastructure"
[Steam Temple, Herman Park] Landscape Narratives:
Design Practices for Telling Stories (New York: John Wiley & Sons, 1998)

KEVIN POWELL, "Suburban Harvest"
[Lee's Orchard Housing, Santa Clara, CA], Landscape Architecture (April 1991)

KEN SMITH, "Linear Landscapes"
Harvard Design Magazine (Winter/Spring 1999)

Dan Solomon, "Beth Israel Chapel"
Places (Fall 1998)

GARY STRANG, "Infrastructure as Landscape"
Places (Summer 1996)

GARY STRANG, "Steam Temple"
Urban Paradise: Gardens in the City (New York: Public Art Fund, 1994)

GARY STRANG, "Notes from Underground"
[Infrastructure], Landscape Architecture (June 1995)

JAMES GRAYSON TRULOVE (ED.), The New American Garden
(New York: Whitney Library of Design, 1998)

ELKE VON RADNIEWSKY, "Quadratur des Gartens"
[Barbara Solomon], Architektur und Wohnen (April-May 1991)

SURRATIONAL LANDSCAPE

The landscape projects of Kathryn Gustafson all exhibit a fascination with sculptural form and sensuous surface – the 'presence of landscape'. This particular quality of her approach to landscape architecture reveals traces of her early training as a textile designer prior to schooling at the Ecole Nationale Supérieure du Paysage de Versailles. The tactile, fluid quality of her work conceals a rigorous organization of space and function most often considered the hallmark of modernist landscape architecture. The work, however, transcends modernist formalism by the signature Gustafson close reading of site and ecology (inclusive of multiple cultural histories). This is, in effect, writing atop the language of modernism a new language that is best described as 'surrational' (after Bachelard).

Gustafson's Imaginary Garden, in the historic village of Terrasson-la-Villedieu (France), included multiple iterations of "garden history" of such delicate scale and impressionistic appeal that the usual pitfalls of episodic form typical of theme parks and historic sites are totally averted. The park includes a virtual time-warp in the form of a glass house (by architect Ian Ritchie) sited in the landscape such that it 'disappears', from above and afar, disguised as a body of shimmering water (glass). The irrigated gabion stone walls enclosing the structure from below further serve to destabilize the typology and produce, instead, an idealized miniature landscape under glass and behind stone (with a decidedly 'archaic' ambiance) – a schema re-visited at a much greater scale in the Great Glass House of the National Botanic Garden, Wales.

Part of the puzzle of surrational creations – poems or landscape gardens – is the presence of undercurrents or dissonant (discordant) elements or qualities that illumine the mind while addressing the eye. One may feel reminded of certain aspects of 1960s concrete poetry: this poetic code remained gnomic due to its abbreviated, yet precise language; it was elliptical and in most cases intensely anagogical, creating a chain of inferences or a series of links or feints to distant or non-existent referents. The surrational sublime has become one of the chief determinants of a very powerful post-cultural consciousness in arts and letters that destabilizes the conventions and codes of the modernist worldview through carefully crafted elisions and aporias reaching beyond the boundaries of the conventional.

249

250

251

252

249 | 250 | 251 | 252
Imaginary Garden with Cultural Greenhouse, Terrasson-la-Villedieu, France

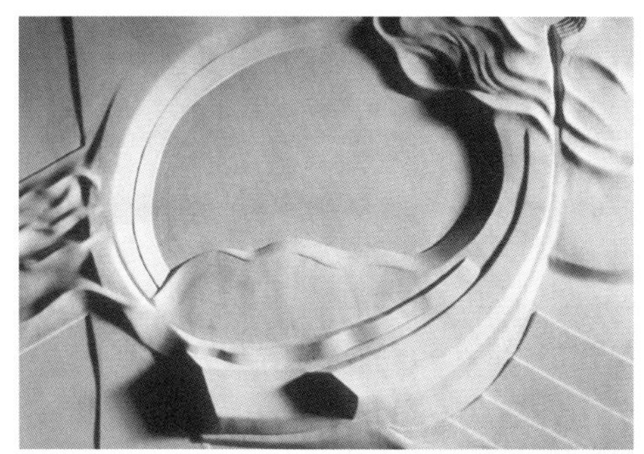
253

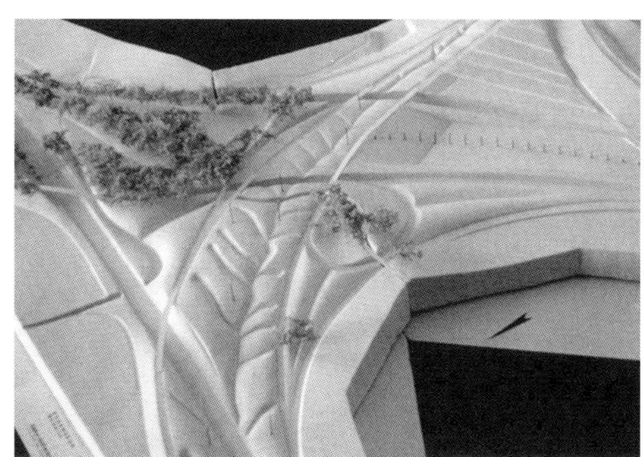
254

255

Kathryn Gustafson's work is clearly an extension and elaboration of issues raised in the heady heyday of land art, a movement of the 1960s–1980s allied with minimalist and post-minimalist art. The primary premises of the movement were highly poetic *and* environmental versus rational *and* artificial. Such categories have since, more or less, fallen by the wayside with the unpredictable and unbridled fusion of the arts of the 1990s. Both the Venice Biennale and Germany's dokumenta have been instrumental in pushing installation art toward the total work of art (*gesamtkunstwerk*), which land art in many ways has long anticipated.

The strategic methodologies employed by Kathryn Gustafson partly account for the poetic content of her designs. Relying on thematic sketches and subtle sculptural models (often first shaped in clay and then cast in plaster), Gustafson elicits from the materials an iconic and symbolic touchstone. This talisman is used throughout the design process and serves as a reference during the more mundane tasks of design development. The models are often scanned by a laser and turned into wire-frame images on a computer for further elaboration.

The process produces proto-environmental and cultural ciphers usually based on an exceptionally spare system of verbal or visual metaphors. These are used to build up meaning within the design process and make connections to larger systems both absent and present. The terse, epigrammatic nature of the terminology allows for the spaces between the terms to build up a 'charge' so-to-speak – an atmospheric current – which leaps from the imagistic matrix into the production of the forms. This intuitional and verbal process relies on a language of both natural and unnatural elements, an amalgam, which is the essence of designed landscape.

253
Morbras,
France,
model (land, water, shadow)

254 | 255
Penne-Mirabeau freeway,
France,
model views

The brief for the National Botanic Garden Great Glass House in Llanarthne, South Wales was quite simple: encompass the widest range of mediterranean plants and systems from South Africa, South Western Australia, Chile, California and the Mediterranean proper as possible. The curators and architect Norman Foster envisioned a 3 500-sq.-m. microcosm of worldwide mediterranean 'ecosystems' (100 000 plants) comfortably enclosed in the 95-m.-long-by-55-m. -wide torpidal dome on the 560-acre grounds of a former historic manor house, Middleton Hall (demolished in the 1950s).

Commissioned as 'interior' landscape architects, Gustafson Porter was not actually responsible for choosing plant materials. They developed a color-height matrix with the Botanic Garden's landscape architect Hal Moggridge to serve as a long-term blueprint for the project, allowing the curators to place plants where they would as long as the plantings conformed to the visual code established in the guidelines. Instead, they focussed their attention on the interior landforms.

Gustafson Porter's model illustrates the 'proto-geological' forms that were to give the glass house a varied and illusory topography. Deep cuts represent ravines and passages below grade increasing the overall maximum interior height to 20 m., from the original preliminary 14 m. These slices in turn serve as occasions to introduce both shear and cascading walls that support plants and, due to the alignment, create shaded and sunny exposures. The sandstone walls are both structural and environmental solutions originating in a schematic overview that sought to create horizon lines within the glasshouse, moving the eye away from the glass structure itself and into the interior landscape. The glass substitutes for sky in this schema, a type of abstraction gained from lowering the landscape and carving up the interior ground plane.

Movement through the glass house is orchestrated in both a formal and an informal manner through the outlay of descending and ascending paths and the use of gravel coursing that indicates both walking and planting surfaces. The calibre of the gravel increases as one moves off the paths and into the collections. Visitors are encouraged to wander around.

Water flows through the interior landscape, both seeping from and cascading over walls culminating in a pool at the lowest level. A bridge, crossing a deep cut in the landscape, serves as an observation deck and is the highest point attainable – for humans – within the mediterranean garden.

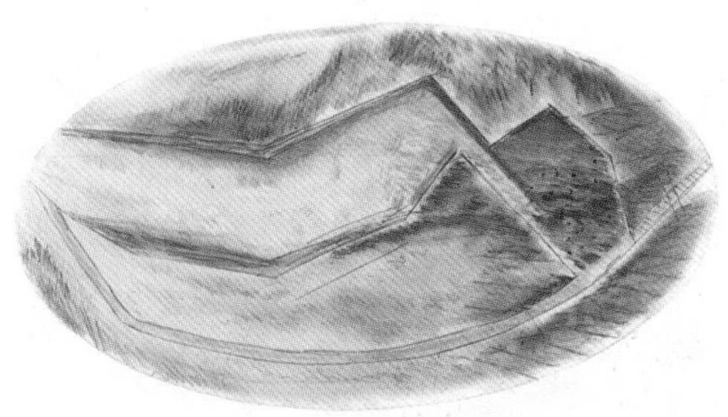

256

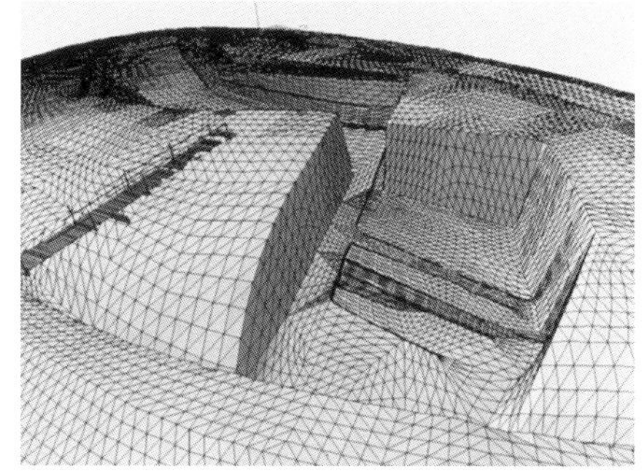

257

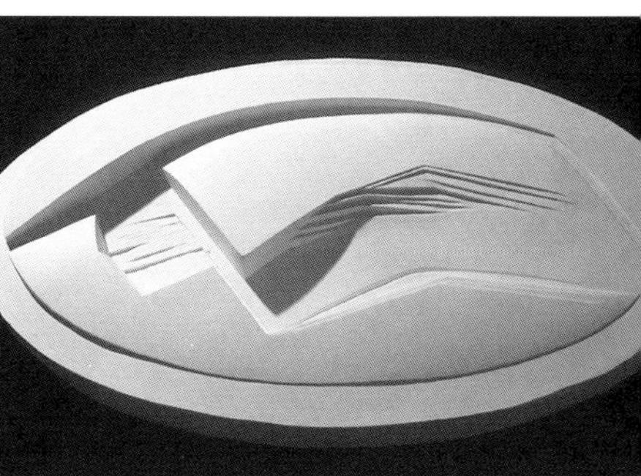

258

259

256
Great Glass House,
Llanarthne,
Wales, Great Britain,
concept sketch

257
Great Glass House,
detail of wire-frame drawing

258
Great Glass House,
model

259
Great Glass House,
shadowed wall slabs

262

263

260

261

260
Great Glass House, gabion sandstone wall and bridge

261
Great Glass House, sandstone 'ravine'

262
Great Glass House, detail of building envelope

263
Great Glass House, in its environment

174

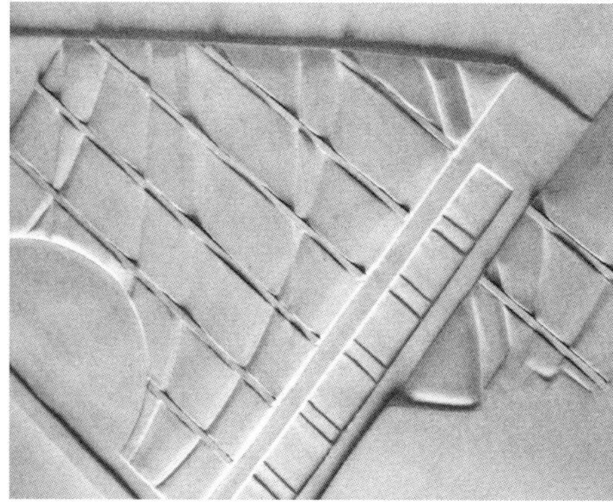

265

ESSO — PARIS, FRANCE

Situated in Rueil, on the banks of the Seine, Esso is the corporate headquarters for the international oil conglomerate Esso / Exxon. The gardens comprise 1 ⅓ acres in the suburban outskirts of Paris.

A chain of visual metaphors 'picture' the cultural and ecological import of the river basin – including the legacy of Impressionism, as represented by La Grande Jatte, an island in the Seine (not far from Esso) where the progenitors of the optical style worked. The landscape imagery is drawn from the rich, verdant nature of the site (those same images that inspired the famous school of painters). Gustafson extracted an associative magic from these cultural forms, playing casually with the atmospheric and terrestrial conditions of the site.

Utilizing a system of canals and a grand water stair, Gustafson linked the building architecture of Viguier & Jodry to the Seine through a descending sequence of channels mediated by the soft silver-green of willow trees and vibrant green grass. The building sits just above the reaches of the 100-year floodtide, and the gentle terraces formed by the canals and stair drop 2 ½ m. to the river.

At the river's edge, above a pedestrian byway, a resting area is provided with Earth Slicers and Water Gazers, two devices of quite different scale for stretching out and enjoying the river view. The Earth Slicer is a ribbon of double-curved rolled steel – fabricated by Paris shipyards. The Water Gazers allow two people to sit facing one another within the concave surface of the steel arcs, as if languishing in a riverside divan.

The canal edges are trimmed with white marble, and slightly raised to provide visual contrast with the darkened grass when the low sun casts shadows across the park. The long center pool (water stair) and the flanking walks are formed out of schist.

264
Esso,
Rueil, Paris, France,
gardens, river,
canal

265
Esso, model

266
Esso,
view through willows

267
Esso, terrace,
overlooking Seine

268
Esso,
water stair

266

267

268

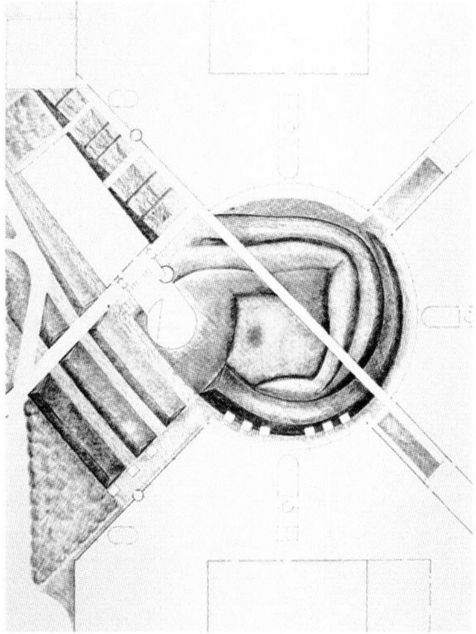

269

L'ORÉAL — PARIS, FRANCE

Using the ambiguous idea of "refinement" as the organizational device for the gardens at L'Oréal, the cosmetics firm, Gustafson created a sequence of three interrelated spaces leading to the inner sanctum of the garden, a lawn and pool. The factory is set in the Aulnay-sous-Bois business park outside Paris and the 1-acre garden is secreted within the form of the Valode & Pistre complex.

The pool is the soulful center of the garden and is planted with water lilies and lotuses. The pool edge is lustrous wood and the darkly mysterious water is a result of painting the concrete base black. The grass mounds, surrounding the central pool, are in part inspired by elements of the human body. The creased fold of the elbow is the physical model for the grass mound that bends as it wraps around the corner of the pool.

The thematic *jouissance* – the joy of inspired refinement – is carried in the movement through the outer layers of the garden, which display somewhat harsher forms and coarser plants, through the bands of roses to the secluded heartland.

Spiraling canals and mounded earth collectively gesture towards the central garden and the planting scheme is elegantly understated once within the center. The center garden is comprised of nine magnolia trees, grass, lilies and lotuses.

269
L'Oréal,
Aulnay-sous-Bois,
Paris, France,
conceptual plan

270
L'Oréal,
water, grass, bridge

271
L'Oréal,
grass 'elbow',
bridge and canal

272
L'Oréal,
pond, copper water wall,
grass mounds

270

271

272

KATHRYN GUSTAFSON | 1 YESLER WAY, SUITE 200 | SEATTLE, WA 98104
T 206 903 6802 | F 206 903 9804

KATHRYN GUSTAFSON trained at the Ecole Nationale Supérieure du Paysage at Versailles, graduating in 1979. Her independent studio projects since 1979 have included parks, urban plazas, roadways, installations and her own private garden on Vashon Island in Puget Sound, near Seattle. Gustafson first came to prominence with her work at Parc de la Villette with Bernard Tschumi. Her association with architects and engineers has provided her with an unusually diverse range of projects that often involve massive earth works. Her œuvre integrates Land Art motives, left over from Minimalist art, and ecological and artistic studies for reprogramming derelict and marginal sites. Her major commissions include corporate campuses for multi-national corporations and urban parks. Gustafson's work with Neil Porter and Ian Ritchie (RFR Architects), both of London, has involved the construction of garden and architectural fabric that blurs the line between professional categories and produces landscape both evocative and discordant.

SELECTED PROJECTS

Western Park
(w/ Gustafson Porter), Amsterdam, Holland, design 2002

Seattle Stadium & Exhibition Center
Seattle, WA, built 2002

Arthur Ross Terrace, American Museum of Natural History
(w/ Anderson & Ray), New York City, NY, built 2000

National Botanic Garden Wales Great Glass House
(w/ Gustafson Porter), Llanarthne, Wales, built 2000

South Coast Plaza
(w/ Anderson Ray), Costa Mesa, CA, built 2000

Imaginary Garden
(w/ Ian Ritchie), Terrasson, France, built 1995

Esso HQ
Rueil, France, built 1992

L'Oréal, Aulnay-sous-Bois
France, built 1992

Human Rights Square
Evry, France, built 1991

Shell Petroleum Company HQ
Rueil-Malmaison, France, built 1991

Morbras
Morbras, France, built 1987

SELECTED BIBLIOGRAPHY

KLAZIEN BRUMMEL, "Kathryn Gustafson wint prijsvraag Westergasfabriek"
Architect (July-August 1997)

LORETTE COHEN, Lausanne Jardins: Une Envie de Ville Heureuse
(Versailles: Editions du Péribole, 1998)

GUY COOPER AND GORDON TAYLOR, Paradise Transformed: The Private Garden for the 21st Century
(New York: Monacelli Press, 1997)

LISA DIEDRICH, "Kathryn Gustafson – Phantasie und Form"
Topos 21 (December 1997)

PAULA DIETZ, "Botanic Garden in Wales Boasts One of World's Largest Glass Spans"
Architectural Record (July 1999)

PAUL FINCH, "Combining Artifice and Nature in the Dordogne"
[Terrasson], Architects' Journal (November 9, 1995)

KATHRYN GUSTAFSON, "Platz der Menschenrechte in Evry"
Topos 10 (March 1995)

MARIELLE HUCLIEZ, Jardins et Parcs Contemporains
(Paris: Telleri, 1998)

RON VAN LEEUWEN, "Glück am Rande: Westergasfabriek in Amsterdam"
Topos 23 (June 1998)

LEAH LEVY, "Kathryn Gustafson: Sculpting the Landscape"
(Washington: Spacemaker Press, 1998)

AXEL SOWA, "Nouvelle Génération de Pylones: RFR Kathryn Gustafson et Ian Ritchie"
L'Architecture d'Aujourd'hui (May 1999)

MAURIZIO VITTA, "Incontrarsi Sotto il Lago"
[Terrasson], L'Arca (September 1996)

PETER WALKER, "Other Directions in Contemporary Landscape Architecture"
[Projects], Space Design (July 1994)

"Ian Ritchie Architects: The Glasshouse Fragment"
[Terrasson], Architectural Design (March-April 1998)

"Imaginärer Kontinent: Gewächshaus-Projekt in Terrasson, Frankreich"
Architektur, Innenarchitektur, Technischer Ausbau (April 1995)

"Inszenierung"
[Lausanne jardins '97], Anthos (February 1997)

273

273
L'Oréal, magnolias

INDEX

ACKNOWLEDGEMENTS

Illustrations are courtesy of the design practices.

COVER
Esso - Kathryn Gustafson

MARPILLERO POLLAK ARCHITECTS
Linda Pollak | 23, 25
Marpillero Pollak | 5, 8, 10, 11, 13, 14, 16, 22, 24

DANADJIEVA & KOENIG
Danadjieva & Koenig | 26, 27, 28, 29, 32, 34, 42, 43, 44
J. F. Housel / DKA | 30, 35, 37, 39, 40
Timothy Hursley / DKA | 31, 36
Darryl Jones / DKA | 33

ANDERSON & RAY
Anderson & Ray | 46, 48, 55, 56
Anderson & Ray / EDAW | 59, 60
Anderson & Ray / Spencer Associates | 61

KEN SMITH LANDSCAPE ARCHITECT
Ron Blunt / KSLA | 63, 64, 65, 66
Betsy Pinover Schiff | 71,72
Ken Smith | 67, 69, 73, 74, 75, 76, 77, 78, 79, 80, 81, 82
Ken Smith / Vogue | 83, 84
Paul Warchol / KSLA | 68

OSLUND & ASSOCIATES
Oslund Associates | 85, 87, 88, 89, 90, 91, 92, 93, 94, 95, 96, 97, 98
Oslund Associates / Mary Miss | 99, 100, 101, 102
Tom Oslund | 86

MICHAEL SORKIN STUDIO
Sorkin Studio | 117

ANDROPOGON ASSOCIATES
Andropogon Associates | 121, 122, 123, 125, 126, 127, 128, 129, 130, 131, 132, 134, 136, 137, 138, 139, 140, 141, 142, 143, 144, 145

BURTON & COMPANY
Burton & Company | 157, 158, 160, 161
Burton & Company / Ashen + Allen | 153
Steve Hug / Burton & Company | 151
Michael Moran / Burton & Company | 146
Philip Steinman | 148, 149

ANDREW SPURLOCK MARTIN POIRIER
Spurlock Poirier | 163, 164, 167, 168, 169, 170, 172, 173, 174, 176, 177, 178, 179, 180, 182, 183
UCSD Stuart Collection | 181

ROMA DESIGN GROUP
Robert Cameron / ROMA | 187
ROMA | 184, 185, 186, 189, 190, 191, 192, 197, 198, 199
San Francisco Examiner / ROMA | 193

ACHVA BENZINBERG STEIN
Achva Stein | 200, 202, 203, 205 209, 210, 218, 219

GARY LEONARD STRANG
Gary Strang | 224, 225, 228, 230, 246, 247, 248
Gary Strang / Michael Roche | 226, 227, 242, 245
Gary Strang / Dan Solomon | 232, 233, 234, 235, 236, 237, 238, 239, 240, 241

KATHRYN GUSTAFSON
Jocelyne van den Bossche / Ian Ritchie Architects | 249, 250, 251, 252
Kathryn Gustafson | 253, 254, 255, 258, 259, 260, 261, 265, 267, 268, 270, 271, 272, 273
National Botanic Garden Wales | 262, 263
Claire de Virieu | 264, 266